FOSTER CHILD

FINDING THE COURAGE TO SUCCEED

DENNIS HARRIS

IUNIVERSE, INC.
NEW YORK   BLOOMINGTON

Foster Child
Finding the Courage to Succeed

iUniverse books may be ordered through booksellers or by contacting:

iUniverse
1663 Liberty Drive
Bloomington, IN 47403
www.iuniverse.com
1-800-Authors (1-800-288-4677)

Because of the dynamic nature of the Internet, any Web addresses or links contained in this book may have changed since publication and may no longer be valid.

ISBN: 978-1-4502-7570-5 (sc)
ISBN: 978-1-4502-7575-0 (dj)
ISBN: 978-1-4502-7574-3 (ebk)

Printed in the United States of America

iUniverse rev. date: 11/29/2010

ACKNOWLEDGEMENTS

I am so grateful to the many people who during my lifetime listened to bits and pieces of my experiences and after allowing me to share with them encouraged me to write a book. I must mention my children, Desiree, Dorian, Donna, Donovan, Danae, David, and Danielle who are the inspiration behind the completion of this project. I have had such a full life experience that included a lot of discouragement which in my opinion has been offset by far more moments of joy. I really have to give credit to the one person who when I was at one of my lowest moments was able to see something in me that made them decide to believe in me. Doris (Peaches) the love of my life has allowed me to explore all of the possibilities for my life without hesitation. She has supported me through the rough patches and has encouraged me on to achievement. Her love for me has been unwavering and I realized long ago just how blessed I am to know her. Through this book project she supported my time away from the family as I toiled to get it completed. She once again showed that same love and patience during the sometimes painful moods that I experienced while recounting the many stressful times in my life journey. To her I say thanks for once again giving me room to achieve.

I have over the years been very careful about the selection of friends and I feel very good about those selections. I am often teased by my young adult children about the small number of friends that I have. What they don't understand is that I cherish quality over quantity. My small groups of friends including Norman, Blake, Dennis, John, Gerald, Reginald, Tyrone (my barber who constantly encourages me to achieve during every haircut), Carmelita, and Walker who serve as part of the inner circle of support to Doris, all have become an integral part of my life and to whom I owe gratitude.

Bessie and Ward…wow your lifelong love and support is immeasurable. My siblings for allowing me to focus on family and career and not putting pressure on me to be a better big or little brother. I thank each of you for your patience with me, loving me in spite of the way I treat you.

Without all of you and the many unnamed but not forgotten supporters I would not have been able to complete this story.

Thank You

CONTENTS

CHAPTER 1

FROM SCOTT TO HARRIS

My daily journey to work takes me down a road that conjures up both physical reminders and emotional memories of my life. Every day, while I sit in traffic on 295, I have plenty of time to dwell on those memories, seeing to my right the former site of D.C. Junior Village, where my mother gave me away, and to my left, the Naval Research Lab, where the father that I never really knew worked for 35 years. Whichever direction I turn, I'm reminded every single day – of my father, of my early childhood years, of my ongoing longing and search for a home, an identity, a family.

The memories and the emotions surface so vividly – while I sit in traffic on 295 or in the middle of the night while I try to sleep – that they catch me off guard sometimes. I remember the physical obstacles and struggles of being born a minority, raised in meager, if not totally inadequate living conditions, and have to remind myself that my present reality is about as far from that as you can get. I reflect back, not only on those tangible hardships, but on the less visible, far more devastating suffering of some of the deepest pain, loneliness and sadness that a person can experience. And I remind myself again that I've not only persevered and survived through it all, I've come out on the other side, risen above it and have something to offer – in spite of or, perhaps because of, the life I was born into.

My story began in 1957 in D.C. General Hospital, the city's only public hospital, which has since closed after serving the area for almost 200 years. In that location now is D.C. General Health Campus, which is made up of several clinics, including Women's Services, Detoxification Center, and Southeast Sexually Transmitted Diseases Clinic.

My grandmother's house in Northwest D.C. is where I lived – 1444 Ogden Street NW.

One of my earliest, most significant childhood memories is reciting my name and that address, over and over again. I guess my mother must have taught me that, like any parent would in case their child should get lost or need help. I chanted "Dennis Alton Scott, 1444 Ogden St., NW," over and over and over again. That was my name, that was where I lived – or so I thought.

My grandmother's house was a boarding house – and not in the greatest of areas at the time. My mother, brothers and sisters, other relatives, and even some people I didn't know occupied rooms there. It's difficult now to imagine living in the same house with people you don't really know, but at such a young age, it didn't really have an impact on me one way or the other.

Since I was younger than five years old, my memories about those days are very vague. I don't recall spending a lot of time with my mother, partly because she worked a lot or perhaps I was just too young to have had much of a relationship with her yet. I do remember feeling so proud of her back then, though. She would get dressed for work every day in a crisp, white uniform. I just naturally thought she was a nurse. In actuality, my mother worked for a service cleaning other people's houses.

When she would get dressed up, and change from her "nurse's" uniform into stockings and high heels, she was an attractive woman. She enjoyed music and dance, and my siblings and I enjoyed listening to the soulful sounds of Sam Cooke and Jerry Butler with her, learning the lyrics and making up dance routines.

My mother was a bit of a partier in her day. We kids looked forward to company visits, because she'd let us dance and perform. We would get so excited when she let us do this; we loved to show what we could do, and craved attention, from anyone who was willing to give it.

Some of those company visits were intended to be more private in nature, I suppose. My mother was a single woman and would, from time to time, enjoy the company of men in the living room, behind closed doors. The door had one of those skeleton lock keyholes, which gave the peeping eyes of my brother and me plenty to view. I was very curious about the things I saw take place through that keyhole. Those visual images impacted me profoundly at a very early age, and I probably had more desire than the average young boy growing up.

Most of the other memories of living at my grandmother's house are dim – except for the time that I almost burned the house down. My older brother and I were home alone, not an unusual occurrence. I generally remember seeing my mother only at night before bedtime. We were striking matches and poking them through the sheer curtains hanging in the dining room, which eventually went up in flames. We were lucky not to have been hurt and fortunately, the house wasn't destroyed.

Leaving young children unattended like that today could land you in jail, or at least, in very big trouble. Thankfully, the mistake my brother and I made was one that we only had to pay for with a spanking. The situation could have been so much worse, though of course we thought it was the end of the world at the time.

That's the only memory I have of my father ever spanking me, not that it wasn't well-deserved.

I saw my father once a week or so for the first five years of my life. He didn't live with us at the boarding house, and wasn't married to my mother. But he did come by every Saturday – or just about. He'd give us a quarter and send the older kids to the store to buy a pack of boloney and a loaf of bread. Believe it or not, that was something special for me and my siblings. Once in awhile, my father would take us on a drive over by Rock Creek Park in Northwest D.C., but I don't recall any specific conversations we ever had. I was, after all, very young.

I had no real connection with this man that I knew to be my father. Some kids have memories of their father teaching them to catch and throw a ball, ride a bike or maybe impart a piece of advice or share a life lesson somewhere along the long road from adolescence to adulthood. Although I know that my father came to see his children every week, I cannot recall a single conversation with him in those early years. In fact, once I was moved from my grandmother's house, I didn't see the man again until I was in my thirties.

I say "once I was moved" because that move, that decision was made for me. At five years old, I certainly wasn't able to make decisions about where I lived, but the move that was forced upon me was not your typical "moving day." Moving is a transition to a new house, new neighbors or a new school. Though that's difficult enough on a young child, there's a certain element of excitement that accompanies it.

My move was far more life-altering. I clearly remember the cab ride. The feelings, even now, are so distinct, yet difficult to put into the right words. I can still picture my mother gathering all of us, her children, into a cab one day and telling us she couldn't take care of us anymore. I was confused and naturally very frightened and upset. .   If my mother wasn't going to take care of me anymore, who was?

Throughout the ride, she coached me to say my name. Over and over again, she made me repeat, "My name is Dennis Harris." Dennis Harris – my new name. This upset and confused me even more. Why couldn't I tell anyone my *real* name – the name I had been accustomed to? Why did I now have to use the last name of my older sister's father?

The car ride with my mother ended at D.C. Junior Village, a city-owned and operated orphanage in Southwest D.C., and my new home. It felt more like I was being sent to jail. To make matters worse, at some point during the ride, my mother made the decision to keep my older sister and my older brother. I was losing my name, my mother, my home, and half of my family. (Really, my entire family, since boys and girls were separated at D.C. Village, and I would rarely end up seeing my younger sisters.)

My life as I knew it vanished in an instant. What I couldn't know at the time – what I wouldn't come to understand for many years – is that terrible, awful things can happen in your life, things that you don't deserve and that aren't your fault, but you can't control them. How you respond to them, when you are capable of responding, is up to you. You can let your past hold you back and retreat into a corner or you can come out swinging, confronting, overcoming and knocking out the obstacles one by one. At five, I wasn't at all capable of controlling what was happening to me.

While being abandoned at the orphanage was bad enough, what was far more devastating was the fact that my mother had made a choice, *and she had not chosen me*. I was so young and so conflicted, asking her over and over, "Why did you choose him?" Wasn't there something in me to make her want to keep *me?* Her logical response, lost on my five-year-old mentality, was that my brother was older and could do more to help her. I felt unworthy and unwanted, like I was being thrown away.

This feeling of not being good enough, of not being the chosen one, is one obstacle I continually have to fight off, even to this day.

But on that day, back in 1962, it was clear that there was no way out. Dennis Alton Scott of 1444 Ogden St., NW, ceased to exist from that moment.

My name was Dennis Harris, and I became a ward of the city of Washington, D.C. on that day.

CHAPTER 2

THE ORPHANAGE

When Hillary Clinton wrote the book, *It Takes a Village*, The D.C. Junior Village is not at all what she was referring to.

The orphanage opened its doors in 1948, and by the time it closed those doors in 1973, it had held more than 900 children. There aren't words adequate enough to explain the feelings of growing up in a home that wasn't a home at all. Back in those days, children basically had no rights. Being too small in both mind and frame, kids could not stand up for themselves and there were no advocates in place at the time to stand up for them.

Along with the rights of other minorities, children's rights have gained much attention in the past couple of decades. And, thanks to laws and regulations about the care of disadvantaged, homeless, underprivileged and underserved children, institutional settings like D.C. Junior Village are, mercifully, a thing of the past.

Jackie Kennedy once visited the orphanage at Christmas time during her husband's presidency – I could very well have been there that day, though I have no memory of it. I just came across that fact online.

What I do remember about D.C. Junior Village are nosebleeds, bedwetting and crying.

The environment of the Junior Village was sterile, cold and prison-like. A scared and lost little boy, I looked at the roads that led in, out and around the Village every day, wondering where they led to, yearning to escape, longing to break out. But I was young and I was helpless. In which direction would I run – and who would I run to? If I did find my way out of this place, where would I go?

That feeling, that need to get away from there, is still as sharp as a razor and cuts deep into my soul. I can still feel it inside of me almost five decades later.

I yearned for my mother. The impact of her loss was devastating on me. Night after night, I cried myself to sleep, banging my head against the cold metal of the bunk bed in which I slept. The dormitories consisted of several rooms with row after row of bunk beds, identical striped mattresses on each one. No cozy comforters or cheery colors, and no consoling arms to tuck you in and hug you goodnight.

These dormitories where the children of the orphanage escaped the harsh reality of their lives through welcome, if not fitful, sleep, were not exactly warm and inviting. But sleep was not much of an escape for me. In fact, I believe I suffered the most emotional damage during bedtime at the orphanage because I was a bedwetter. The counselors had real issues with that. I don't know what caused my problem, but I know that I had no control over it. Wetting the bed was a daily fear for me that I worried about constantly, and tried so hard to keep from happening. My anxiety was even worse because of the reaction my problem evoked from the counselors. I wanted to crawl into a hole. Or, not exist. I felt very little in those moments. I remember feeling, even back then, that their reaction to my bedwetting was harsh and hardhearted.

Why couldn't they be more understanding about my bedwetting or my nose bleeds? These things weren't my fault. I didn't want them to happen, and they just added to the sense of feeling like I was being held captive. Another situation I was powerless to do anything about. This went on every single day for the entire time I lived at the orphanage. Those difficult and embarrassing nights were very damaging to my self-esteem. I didn't know then how I would ever get through it, but my bedwetting stopped the day I went into foster care.

A bit like prisoners, the children in the orphanage had to follow set routines. Counselors supervised our every move, from getting dressed in the morning to marching us in for breakfast, then to school and back to our rooms. Everything was self-contained at D.C. Junior Village.

Everything you needed was there. Well, everything the city decided orphans needed, anyway. An infirmary, an elementary school, a dining hall, and of course, the dormitories where we lived, were all on the grounds. It was a very institutional setting.

Being physically cared for isn't the same as being raised with nurturing, love and values. Fortunately, somewhere way down the line some basic human instincts kicked in and I discovered that I could give my own children the kind of childhood I hadn't even been able to imagine as a child.

The living arrangements at the orphanage were determined by age and sex. The buildings that my sisters and I lived in were divided by a long field with playground equipment on it. The girls' dorm was at the base of a hill. Though I would see them almost every week during visitation hour, I don't remember us interacting very much. Neither do my sisters. Our relationships did not develop during those years. I guess we were separated in a lot of different ways, not just by the dorms we lived in.

Only once, in the far too many years I spent in that orphanage, did I have a fleeting moment of feeling on top of the world. I was in third grade, and had practiced my multiplication tables very hard in preparation for class. I got them all right! This was a rare event, and it felt odd for me. I was actually being praised, and it made me feel really good that my teacher made such a big deal out of my accomplishment. It was the first time ever that I had been given so much approval. .

This teacher left me in charge of the class when she was called out of the classroom a short while later. A reward for my having done such a good job. I took this responsibility far too seriously, but never having been recognized for anything in my life, I guess I wanted to make the most of my moment. Once she left the room, the other students teased and made fun of me. In a split second, my moment was crushed. Feeling humiliated, I picked up a chair and angrily flung it wildly, in no particular direction.

Instead of being on top of the world, I ended up in detention. I've since dealt with the rage and tantrums of many children, my own included, and know that patience and reassurance, along with a firm reprimand, can convey a much greater lesson and build confidence rather than break it down,

That incident is my most vivid memory of D.C. Junior Village.

I'd all but forgotten that my mother would come to visit during Sunday visitation days. I was physically there during those visits, but in a sense, I wasn't really there at all. I can't remember feeling excited about seeing her. The woman I longed for and begged not to leave me – and yet I don't recall any emotion attached to her visits. Those were strange moments, in retrospect.

The older kids who lived at the orphanage certainly had my attention. I thought I would be just like them one day. Luckily, that never happened. But at that time, to a young adolescent, those teenage boys seemed to be so cool. I longed to be older, like them. In my eyes, they had themselves together and knew where they were going. I thought they were in control. It's almost funny that I looked at those boys that way when I was younger. And, sad.

Those years were the loneliest and most difficult years of my life. There were hundreds of kids living at D.C. Junior Village, yet, to this day, I cannot recall a relationship with anyone during the entire time I lived at the orphanage. I can't recall a single face. I can't remember the names of any of the counselors. I can't recall a fight. No one stands out in my memory. I cannot recall a single thing that connects me to another person during that time period. Nothing. What I do remember quite well are the feelings of complete isolation and loneliness.

CHAPTER 3

A Foster Home

The event that I still believe has had the greatest impact on my life happened when I was nine years old. My social worker came to my dorm at D.C. Junior Village, took me into a separate room, and told me that she had good news. She had a place for me to go, as in a home. A foster home.

It's difficult to describe what I felt upon hearing this news. I'd lived at the orphanage for so long, and don't even know whether I consciously thought any longer about the day when I'd be able to leave. All those roads I used to look at when I first arrived had become just part of the landscape; they had lost their appeal as escape routes.

I don't recall if I asked about my sisters at the time. Although we were all there at the orphanage, I don't think our interaction was a big factor in my life. Or maybe, like everything else that had happened to me, there was no point in my feeling one way or another. The decisions, the choices, were not in my own hands. Every single thing about my life was decided by other people.

The social worker helped me to pack up my things, and that very same day, I left the orphanage. I was still a child, and so I was simply excited about the fact that I was going somewhere, though I'm sure I didn't really understand what it all meant. I got into the social worker's government issued vehicle – a cold, impersonal car that felt more like a police car. I recall that she had me sit up front and didn't even buckle my seatbelt. How times have changed….You'll get a ticket for something like that now, though plenty of things I experienced in my childhood would be considered against the law today, or at the very least, abuse or neglect.

We drove from Southeast D.C. to Northeast D.C., which meant nothing to me, since I had no bearings, had never really been anywhere and didn't understand the city. But I was, in essence, going from a poorer side of town to a nice, middle-class, residential neighborhood. Okay, maybe lower-middle-class, but certainly a few steps up from where I was coming from.

We pulled up in front of a single-family house surrounded by green hedges that looked like a fence. As we sat out front, still in the car, I asked the social worker the name of the family I was about to live with. I struggled with the name, repeating it over and over. I'm not sure why. Rollins doesn't seem to be such a difficult name to remember. Maybe it had something to do with my own name change that took place in another vehicle four or five years earlier. I really don't know.

Then I asked, "Why did they pick me?" The social worker reached into her purse, retrieved a photo of me and told me that Mr. and Mrs. Rollins had seen my picture and thought I would fit well into their family. That sounded so strange, so odd to me. Someone decided they wanted me by looking at my picture. How could my appearance alone be enough to persuade a family to take me in? Did it mean that who I really was, on the inside, didn't even matter?

My introduction to Mr. and Mrs. Rollins was sort of formal. I learned that they had four other foster children, all siblings, who were at school when I first got to the house. Their other little girl, Doreen, was a toddler they had adopted at birth.

I was the second oldest in this mix of now six children living in the Rollins' home, and was one of two boys. I remember well being shown my room, which I shared with the other boy. At my grandmother's, we had all slept in one bedroom; at the orphanage, there were rows and rows of bunks. Here, there were two beds, two dressers, a window, and space. For the first time in my life, I felt like I had my own room.

As I lived with Mr. and Mrs. Rollins, I grew to understand who they were and where they had come from. Within only months, I was referring to them as "mom" and "dad." Did this stem from any particular feelings of closeness or warmth that I felt for them? I really can't say. It might just have been because all of the other kids in the house called them that. For whatever reason, I began using those terms early on.

Naturally, the honeymoon period ended after a while. While I was happy to be part of a family at last, there was a learning curve that kids born into families don't necessarily experience. Adapting to new rules time and again throughout my life instilled a sense of discipline in me; sometimes challenging those rules inspired strength and courage.

As a member of their household I was, of course, expected to do things according to their rules. I didn't really understand the Rollins' mentality during the nine years that I lived there, but now, as an adult, I give them a lot of room for error considering all the circumstances.

Mr. Rollins was illiterate. He could not read or even write his own name. Mrs. Rollins had an eighth-grade education. He was a farmer from Louisa County, Virginia; she grew up in a little city just outside of Birmingham, Alabama. They were raised in a certain way, worked hard together and amassed enough to own their own single-family home in a relatively nice D.C. neighborhood. I came to understand later that their participation in the foster care program was, to a degree, related to the fact that it was their major source of income.

Mrs. Rollins was the true country housewife and homemaker. She cooked big meals from scratch every night. Food was never an issue; there was always an abundance of food and drink. Nothing went to waste; she even used coffee grounds boiled on the stove top to make fresh coffee.

I got my love of cooking from Mrs. Rollins and learned a lot in her kitchen.

There was a constant fight between "mom and dad" about whether their other "son" and I should be in the house, learning cooking and other domestic skills, or outside farming. Here we lived in this urban D.C. area, 30th St, NE – what is now known as the Fort Lincoln area – and we were literally farming. Mr. Rollins actually had a tractor and would plow the grounds, a couple of acres worth of land, to grow crops of corn, potatoes – all kinds of vegetables. The neighbors on either side even allowed him to farm their land that was attached. At one point, we even had livestock.

So, in this Northeast D.C. neighborhood, where I played street football out in front of my house with other boys my age, I was also a farmer, walking the plow. I got teased about it a lot, but I bear no resentment about the work I did out there. I learned from Mr. Rollins how to work *really* hard. At 9, 10, 11 years old, I was trimming hedges that went all the way around the house and mowing about a quarter of the land they owned. Hard work was important to him – to both of them. It was part of their upbringing and their values, and they passed that work ethic on to me. I believe it has served me well throughout my life.

Had working hard not been instilled in me early on in, I'm fairly certain I would not have achieved the success I have as a businessman today. But, that silver lining wasn't immediately visible to me back then.

There were definitely times when I did not at all appreciate Mr. Rollins' ethics and values. For one thing, he had no tolerance for mistakes. When I struggled to hold the plow, couldn't keep up or keep the rows straight, he would jump off the tractor and smack me upside the head. This type of reaction happened routinely, and not only to me.

It wasn't unusual for all of the children in the house to get beatings. We'd even have to go out and cut the switch that they'd beat us with from the tree. In retrospect, I'm sure some of those beatings were well deserved. But I'm not so sure about others. I recall once sitting at the dinner table, shaking salt into my bowl of beans. We weren't supposed to do this ourselves, but let Mr. or Mrs. Rollins do it for us. I figured I was old enough to shake my own salt, and of course, the top came off the salt shaker and all this salt came spilling down into my beans. My foster father made me eat that entire bowl. I threw up all over the place, while I was still eating. Of course, I got whipped and had to clean it up. To this day, I do not like salt. And I still think that beating was an overreaction to spilled salt.

A lot of emotion and commotion went into the dynamics of my relationship with my foster parents. They are so much a part of the story of my life. In a sense, they helped to shape my image of the person and parent I eventually wanted to be, which did not emulate them very much at all. Mr. and Mrs. Rollins were a bit rough around the edges, and not in any way supportive of things like helping with homework or involving me in activities.

At one point, my foster parents did make a petition to adopt me. Part of the process for adoption required that my mother reach out to see if that was something I wanted. A lot of kids might have jumped at the chance to become a "real" member of the family, but I had a mother. Although I'd lived in D.C. Village for so long, I wasn't an orphan. And though I was grateful for a place to live, I still had a family of my own – somewhere.

During that time, my mother called to say that she wanted me to take on my birth name, Dennis Alton Scott, again. I told her I thought it was a crazy idea to change my name, and refused to do it. That phone call was pretty much the extent of my preteen and teen relationship with my mother. I did not talk to her again until I was 35 years old.

While it seems odd for me to take a stand to keep a name I knew did not belong to me, everyone in my life knew me as Dennis Harris. Being 13 can be difficult enough for a kid; changing my identity – again – just seemed like adding more confusion to an already confusing age. And it didn't make sense to me to change my name and then have to explain everything to all the people who already knew me – teachers, friends, classmates, churchgoers. My name was Dennis Harris.

CHAPTER 4

SUMMER TIMES

Nearly every summer that I lived with the Rollins', the family went on a road trip. In all the time I knew them, the only car they ever drove was a station wagon; if they bought a new car, it was sure to be a station wagon. For some reason, I always felt funny about riding in one. I felt like we were so conspicuous, this big group of people in a silly-looking car.

Sometimes we'd go to Mr. Rollins' home town in Louisa County, Virginia, which I thought then was such a long way, although now people from D.C. go there to shop. It was very rural, "down the country" as we called it. Other times we took even longer trips to Birmingham, Alabama, where Mrs. Rollins was born.

One summer, around 1969 or '70, we headed to Alabama. We were going to the town of Carrollton, which was very rural – there was an outhouse and we had to use chamber pots at night. I remember sitting on the porch, watching people chew snuff.

This was not too long after Dr. Martin Luther King Jr. had been assassinated, and though I was aware, I didn't really understand the ramifications at that point. When we drove by the courthouse, Mrs. Rollins pulled over and told us about the legend of an African-American man named Henry Wells, who had been accused of burning it down in the late 1800's. The townspeople lynched him, but not before he threatened to haunt the town forever. Mrs. Rollins told us that we'd see his image in the window. Even though they'd changed the windows, Henry's image was still visible.

I was about 11 or 12, and that story made a lasting impression. Yet when I tell my own children about it, they just blow it off. They have very little connection to the civil rights movement; to them it's a story in a book.

On the one hand, I think that lack of connection to one's history is sad. Countless sacrifices have been made by so many people, regardless of race, creed or stature, to support a cause, perpetuate a movement, share a dream and make a difference. To not acknowledge those sacrifices is akin to not honoring them. On the other hand, the fact that my own children, and all the children of this generation, can't relate to this period of racial prejudice, discrimination and suppression means that we, as a people, have indeed overcome many of those injustices.

As for me, growing up in an orphanage and then in a foster home, the obstacles I needed to overcome were far more personal, definitely challenging, and sometimes seemingly insurmountable. But, I think being exposed to the different ways that people live their lives – me, the Rollins', their family in Alabama and Virginia, the people I met in school and in my neighborhood – I learned something early on about perseverance and making the most of both good opportunities and bad situations. I didn't always do it right, but I tried to pay enough attention to the things that made some sort of impression on me.

I guess that's how I ended up playing tennis. Summers were long and dull at the Rollins' home. There wasn't much to do besides the always-present farm work, so any escape was welcome. The day-camp program at Langdon Park offered the perfect opportunity for youths in the community to occupy their time while school was out. This neighborhood recreation center was a fairly large one and included an outdoor pool – one of the few centers that had one – a playground and a basketball court. I'm not sure how I ended up at that day-camp. I doubt the Rollins' actually enrolled me; I may have just wandered over there and never left.

At the beginning of my first summer at Langdon Park, I spent most of my time just hanging around. I had no real purpose, other than to be away from the farm work that awaited me at the Rollins' home. I was more or less idle at the camp, and uninvolved in any of the activities, until the fateful day that I wandered over to the tennis courts. I had been hanging out in the pool area for awhile. The tennis courts were a distance away, and I decided to hang out there for a change of scenery and watch kids my own age playing tennis. They were part of the National Junior Tennis League, a program co-founded by the African-American tennis star, Arthur Ashe, to serve underprivileged children by offering low-cost tennis and life skills instruction. His belief was that, "Through tennis, lives can be changed and spirits reclaimed."

I have to say that Mr. Ashe was right. Being exposed to the game of tennis indeed made quite the change in my life, in more ways than one.

Initially, I would really just get in the way, running onto the court and disrupting the kids and coaches who were out there. After several days of this, the head coach pulled me to the side. I suppose he could have scolded me, threatened me or banned me from the area, but instead, he *included* me. Basically, the deal was that if I was going to continue to hang around there, I was going to learn how to play tennis. Although I had no racquet, and knew the Rollins' would never spring for one, that coach took care of me, stuck a wood racquet in my hand and began teaching me to play. I was around 11 years old at this time, and really got into the sport.

By the next summer, my tennis skills had really kicked in, and I was full steam ahead and excited to continue playing. My foster parents didn't share my excitement, thought it was a waste of time and certainly would have preferred that I stay around the house and work instead. But I walked the seven blocks to Langdon Park Recreation Center every day, no matter how hot it was outside, and ended up getting pretty good over the years. The coach put me on the tennis team and I participated in actual tournaments against other teams in the league.

When I was 13, my tennis team went to the Citywide Championship. We needed to win one more game to emerge victorious, and mine was the last match played for the championship. Though I had fallen off my bike the week before and hurt my hand pretty badly, I won the game, and we won that championship. It was a special moment, but it was accompanied by the introduction of something else into my life, that would not serve me as well as tennis had.

After the big championship win, our head coach hosted a party at his home to celebrate our victory. As if that wasn't exciting enough, this man was studying for his law degree at Georgetown University and lived right in Georgetown. This was a huge thing to wrap my young, underprivileged mind around. Only a few years earlier, the only life I knew wasn't really a life at all. It was barely an existence. And here I was, winning a championship, celebrating in an upscale environment like Georgetown. I felt like I was well on my way to being where I wanted to be. The coach who had put that racket in my young, inexperienced hand years earlier had no idea of the spirit that he had awakened. A word of praise here, a skill there can be the difference between a child leading a life of value or one that lacks real meaning. At some point, though, a child has to claim responsibility for their own life and their spirit.

That celebration party was spectacular in my eyes. With lots of people, plenty of food and music, I felt like I had finally arrived. I was it.

One of the assistant coaches was a student working at the camp as part of the city's summer jobs program. He was a very popular high school baseball player; that guy everybody thinks is so cool. Of course, I was overly impressed, looked up to him, and wanted to follow him around. I wanted to be like him.

When he asked if I wanted to take a walk, I jumped at the chance to hang out with him. On that stroll through an upper-middle-class Georgetown neighborhood, I was exposed to illegal drugs for the very first time. My "hero" assistant coach pulled a joint out of his pocket and lit it up. He inhaled it, and passed it to me. Wanting so badly to emulate him, I took it without hesitation – smoked and choked. But, I remember that silly feeling, and I remember liking it.

I had just finished my last year at Woodridge Elementary School and would be entering Taft Junior High in the fall. By the end of that summer, I was trying out figure out how to get my hands on some marijuana again.

Fortunately, or as it turns out, unfortunately, I knew that the guys in my neighborhood could hook me up. They were older than me, and laughed at me when I first asked, but I had scraped up enough money to buy a nickel bag of pot from them, and that $5 was all they cared about. I entered middle school that fall so proud that I was the first one amongst my peers who had anything to do with marijuana. I learned how to roll a joint, light it and smoke it. And now, I wanted to get other people into it.

It's not so easy to look back and acknowledge some of the poor decisions I began to make at that point in my life. Maybe, for once, I felt like a "leader." But I chose the wrong path to lead people on. Instead of using the positive skills I'd learned from playing tennis, I chose the other road, the one that couldn't possibly lead me – or anyone – to anyplace good. I was the first in my group to smoke pot; I could be the one to let other people know about what I'd discovered. That choice cost me more than I could have imagined.

The first person I introduced to smoking marijuana was the girlfriend of my best friend, Michael Jones. Michael and his family lived across the street from the Rollins' house. During my first week of living with my foster parents, while I was sitting outside on the stoop, alone and trying to adjust, Michael had walked over, introduced himself, and connected with me in an instant. Before that day, I had never made any connection with anyone my own age. That was the first time – and I was nine years old.

Michael really had no idea of where I was coming from and where I'd been. He was being raised by his parents – both his mother and his father, under the same roof. But, there was no evidence of the differences between our lives. His parents were wonderful and treated me like their own son. His mom would make what seemed to me like the biggest hamburgers I'd ever seen in my life. We devoured them – I remember eating until I felt so full I didn't think I could walk.

We'd have sleepovers, always at his house, of course, and when we didn't, we'd do Morse code, or attempt to, with flashlights shining into each other's bedrooms across the street. We got that idea from reading The Hardy Boys mystery books. Michael had the whole Hardy Boys collection, and he introduced me to the concept of reading as a hobby rather than a necessary evil. We would read the books, and act them out when we could.

We joined Boy Scouts together. We were so very close growing up; we'd shop together, buy the same kind of shoes, go to the same stores. I knew his family – his cousins, aunts and uncles. I always thought we'd be best friends for life.

There were only two things that Michael and I didn't do together. One was play tennis. His parents did things with him over the summer, so he wasn't around to go to Langdon Park with me. The other was drugs. Once I started down the drug path, we began to go our separate ways. Our first fight was over my introducing pot to his girlfriend. She and I smoked some out in the playground of Taft Junior High, and she got sick from it. When he found out that it was me who instigated the situation, Michael wanted to fight me. That was the beginning of the end of our friendship as we knew it.

I spent more and more time with guys from the neighborhood who were into the same bad things I was. And, while I was hanging with the thugs and thinking I'm cool, Michael continued to get good grades and stayed on the college track.

We did communicate a couple of times through the years, and he even still referred to me as his brother 20 years later at his mother's funeral. In that moment, sitting in the same house that I lived across the street from and spent so much time in, it was painful to recall both the good and the bad memories. We never did manage to reconnect after that – I suppose life and the priorities of the present get in the way.

CHAPTER 5

MIDDLE SCHOOL – LEADING A DOUBLE LIFE

While I was losing my friendship with Michael, I was also losing myself along the way. Of course, I didn't realize that at all at the time. I was too wrapped up in my own new-found drug hobby to be aware of what was happening.

I was only in middle school, yet I was smoking, and even stealing whiskey from my foster parents. Old Crow was its name. Imagine drinking something with a name like that – could it possibly taste good? But at that point, the taste wasn't what I was after. I was already looking for ways to alter my consciousness, even at that young age. I'd steal the whiskey, pour it into a baby's bottle and keep it in my locker at school, drinking from it throughout the day – *in middle school*.

I was a decent enough student, even with the drugs and alcohol, getting mostly B's and C's. If I tried at all and paid attention, I could get an A. But I had that edge where I *wanted* to be bad. I was attracted to an element that wasn't good. And I wasn't naïve or stupid – I *knew* what I was doing, if not why I was doing it. Maybe I was searching for something. I was a good kid with a lot of bad things going on.

I was, in a sense, leading a sort of double life. During my years at Taft Junior High School, I attended church every Sunday, either with my foster parents and family, or as I got older, with friends. Asbury United Methodist Church, located in downtown D.C., is a middle class African-American church that is rich with history. Organized in 1836, the first church was a small white frame structure. The church has occupied the same site, on the corner of 11th and K Streets, ever since, and in 1864 established itself as a church for the black congregation with the appointment of its first black pastor. It is on the District of Columbia Register of Historic Places and, in 2003, was approved for listing on the National Underground Railroad Network to Freedom.

The church was a true haven for me. There, I was surrounded by good things and positive influences. The pastor, Rev. Frank L. Williams, would invite me to visit, and I became friends with his son, Mark, who was the same age as me. I think it may have been Mark who convinced me to join the church gospel choir. At the time, it was led by a renowned choir leader who set out to shape and mold us into a well-known, prominent choir. And she succeeded. We even traveled to other churches as a guest choir, and other churches visited our parish as well. If you know my voice and you know anything about music, you'll not be surprised to learn that I was assigned to sing baritone as part of the tenor group. There were four of us in that group – Mark Williams, Mark Jackson, Willy Jolly and I developed a pretty close bond. Willy, by the way, is now a famous motivational speaker and author.

As The Four Tenors, we thought we were pretty talented. The church put on a talent show every year, and naturally we decided to form a group and participate in the show. We practiced for months, every Saturday, always at one of their houses, though never at mine. Unlike the Rollins', their parents were all very supportive of this. We not only rehearsed a popular Jackson Five song, but came up with a dance routine as well - and even outfits. "I'll Be There" was our signature song. We even had microphones.

We gave our group a name. The Four Tenors from Asbury United Methodist Choir became The Mystic Four. I have no idea why we chose that name, but I guess we figured it fit us somehow. On the evening of the talent show, we didn't know that the church had invited another church from out of town to attend the performance. It was a group of Caucasian teenagers from Indiana. When we were announced, we ran out onto the stage in our black shirts, white gloves and white pants. The black lighting made our outfits glow on the stage. We thought we were so cool, and the crowd just went crazy, screaming like we were the real deal. The real Jackson Five. We even got an encore. It was one of the biggest thrills of my life. We went on from there to dabble in performing for awhile, but it didn't last long. I guess we were too young, and without any real guidance about how to promote ourselves, and four strong young egos at play, it wasn't really going to last.

For a period of time, I was really living the church life, but the drugs and the bad influences were still a part of me, too. But the people there didn't know me that way. I would walk across the street from junior high to the pastor's house and hang out with the pastor's son. When I wasn't there, they didn't know that I was off doing things they wouldn't have approved of.

I still see that period as me being in a dark, lonely, lost, searching mode. In retrospect, that's probably a normal feeling for any teenager at that age, but I felt it so strongly. I really believed that no one else had the same feelings, that the circumstances of my life until that point gave me license to practice bad behavior.

In addition to these feelings, I was also experiencing other feelings that were probably very normal for a teenage boy, though I believe that the activities I had seen my mother engaging in strongly increased my curiosity about girls and sex.

The only difference between me and other 13-14 year-old boys was that I was in a real hurry to get to the point of activity that I had witnessed my mother at when I was younger. I think I had an extreme degree of curiosity regarding sexual activity at that age, probably because I had actually seen it for myself. Even in choir, even in church, I was seeking out the girls. The other things that happened as a result ended up being positive and good experiences for me, but the girls were really the main attraction.

Choir always held social events, and at every single one of them I attempted to get a girlfriend, always without success. None of the girls seemed to be as attracted to me as I was to them – maybe I was just too eager. I still remember my first slow dance with a girl, and admit that I got carried away. That dance marked the true beginning of my seeking a relationship with a girl.

That can be one lonely search, which is how I felt throughout so much of my childhood. I recall getting ready for the end of the year school dance before my graduation from Taft Junior High. It was a bit like a prom for middle-schoolers. Though I was involved in so many activities and events, behind all of it, I still felt very much on my own. Remember, I didn't have much support from my foster parents for these types of activities. Knowing that all the other kids would be getting dressed up for the dance, I bought myself a brand new outfit with the money I made working at McDonald's – walking to work in the evenings and on weekends to earn my own money in middle school.

Michael and I went to Flagg Brothers, which sold all the latest styles of shoes. Not fashion sneakers like the kids today would buy, but real dress shoes. I bought a pair of white stacked heels to go with my white slacks and a silky, flowery, red and white dress shirt, which was called a baseball shirt back then. I loved that outfit. I thought I was so cool.

All the while I was at home getting dressed for the dance in my brand new clothes, I kept thinking about how I was actually going to get there. The school was fifteen blocks away. I had no alternative, and walked those fifteen blocks, all dressed up and feeling very much alone. It didn't help to see everyone else's parents dropping their kids off when I got there.

Of course, I smoked a joint on my way to the dance, so by the time I arrived I was feeling ready to party. And all those girls looked so fine to me. I couldn't wait to dance with them. I think I danced most of the night. The Jackson Five, Sly and the Family Stone, James Brown, Ike and Tina – all those songs had us moving. And the slow songs, the ones I looked forward to – even slow-dancing to Marvin Gaye and Barry White, I still went home without a girlfriend!

It's funny now to think that here we were, probably a hundred kids, dancing like crazy in this big, stuffy, hot auditorium. And no one minded. We didn't have the luxury of air-conditioned schools back then, and never even thought about the heat. We were kids, we were there to have fun – and that's exactly what we did. Just another way times have changed, I guess – today a school would cancel the dance if the AC wasn't working.

That summer before high school, I continued to play tennis and work at McDonald's. I remained in the choir right up until I started high school. But I also continued my interest in drugs, which led me to pull away from my participation in the choir and in church.

In 1973, I began my high school years at McKinley Tech, and I took my drug habit with me. Why wouldn't I? By this time, it had simply become a part of who I was. Even while I was in Boy Scouts or on church trips, it was there. I once smoked pot in the bathroom of the bus on a church trip to Hershey, PA. Everyone could smell it; I don't know why I thought they wouldn't. Talk about feeling isolated. It was a church trip and it was clear to me that I was becoming a real outcast. But that didn't stop me. Maybe I was so used to feeling isolated and alone that it was just more of what I considered normal.

Looking back, I'm amazed that I got away with so much. How did no one at my school ever notice that I was drunk or high? Not a teacher, not a classmate, not a counselor – didn't anyone smell liquor on my breath, or see that I was clearly altered? Why didn't anyone on that church bus call me on the fact that I'd just smoked pot in the bathroom?

Now, I'm not laying blame for my behavior on anyone but myself. But I do wonder whether I'd have changed my ways if someone had made me face what I was doing. Although, maybe things happened exactly the way they were supposed to. Maybe no one tried to get me to stop because I was meant to go through those experiences. If you believe, as I do, that every step along your path, and the way you react to what you face, makes you the person you are today, then I guess it all unfolded the way it had to.

CHAPTER 6

LIFE LESSONS

By the time I was in high school, I was a bona fide drug dealer. But I broke the cardinal rule – I was also a *drug user*. Anyone involved with drugs can tell you, you're not supposed to use the stuff if you deal it. Of course, this put me into an even worse situation. I always felt outside and lost, no matter what environment I was in. Even with the people I sold drugs to, I wasn't on the same level with them because I was high, too. I'm not sure I ever got past that feeling – always thinking about everything I've been through and trying to figure out where I fit in and belong.

Just like the people at school and church, my foster parents never did seem to figure out the things I was doing. With the exception of one of my foster siblings, who was also smoking pot, no one else in the house knew either. I'm sure that some of my interactions with them and my reactions to them were influenced by whatever I had been drinking or smoking that day, but no one noticed. As a parent, I can't imagine not being able to tell if one of my kids had been drinking or smoking – but maybe that's just because I know the signs all too well. Or maybe it's because their lives, their behaviors, their overall well-being mean more to me than my life ever meant to anyone when I was their age.

Though the Rollins were far from model parents, and smoked cigarettes and drank, they did it in the context of being adults. It simply wasn't for kids, and I doubt they would ever have thought about any one of us doing those things. They always had a distinct line about the difference between a child's place and an adult's place. In fact, their sayings remain in my head to this day. It's amazing to me how I thought that I wasn't really connected to them, yet I can so easily replicate what I saw every day for all those years. For example, if I asked for an allowance for a chore I'd done, Mr. Rollins always said, "You live here and you eat here, don't you?" I do use that one on my own son today, every now and then, but he doesn't really get it. He just asks me again for more money, something I knew never to do. But it's just an example of how your environment really does shape a part of who you become.

The Rollins also believed that "children should be seen and not heard." They wanted us to sit and look cute if they had company, but we weren't supposed to say a word. My foster parents would actually smack us in front of company if we said something. I can't even imagine doing that; what parent could? It's just so different today, with my children and with my whole generation. We're way on the other side of that kind of thinking. My kids are free-minded. Sometimes they'll use their manners and say "excuse me," but most of the time they just join right in as if they're adults.

I always looked at the Rollins' as being good citizens who tried to do the right thing. Although they weren't educated people, they watched the news on TV and were aware of what was going on both around the country and in our neighborhood. They supported Walter Washington, the first black mayor of Washington, D.C. In fact, he was the first mayor of D.C. ever, having been appointed by President Johnson in 1967. Until then, the city had been under the rule of Congress.

They were certainly aware of the racial problems in D.C., and I recall hearing them talk about Vietnam, shaking their heads over the nightly reports about the dead and wounded troops. I don't think they were in any way trying to shield us children from harsh realities, but they didn't talk about these things with us. I think it was just another instance of their belief that these were adult topics that needn't concern us.

Little did they know that I was involved in behavior that should have been way beyond my experience. Maybe if that line between adult and child had been blurred, even just a little, things might have been different.

Ironically, many years later, after my foster father had passed, it was rumored that my foster mother actually became a drug user. In her mid sixties…life is so unpredictable. I'm not sure how things like that happen, but perhaps Mr. Rollins was so instrumental in her life that when he died, she was just too vulnerable. I was never able to substantiate those rumors although her new friends did appear to be a little shady. I think of her as an example of how you really can reclaim the true goodness within you, in spite of getting sidetracked. Mrs. Rollins was inherently a good woman, and she was able to come out on the other side of her own darkness, back to the light within.

Because of some of the experiences I had with the Rollins family, I made a commitment to myself about the way I would raise and treat my own children when the time came. I vowed to raise my children differently, and value things like education and enrichment activities like dance, karate, basketball and tennis. Mr. & Mrs. Rollins had a lot to do with the kind of parent I wanted to be – and *didn't* want to be. I vowed that I would not treat my family the way the Rollins' treated me and my foster brother and sisters.

There were instances and incidents, two in particular, that motivated me to actually physically fight back. Mr. Rollins once hit me and knocked me down with a shovel; another time, he grabbed me in a headlock and busted my ear. For days afterward, I slept with a small-handled ax that I had from Boy Scouts beneath my pillow. Then, I made up my mind that I was going to learn to fight so I could protect myself.

Early during my tenth-grade year at McKinley, I approached the coach of the boxing team at school about joining up. He told me I had to try out in order to be on the team. I was on a mission, thinking that if my foster father ever touched me again, *I* was going to beat *him*. I worked out vigorously, running in the mornings with other team members, and practicing with them. I ended up being pretty good at boxing and made the team. I wonder now whether I was subconsciously addressing any other aggressions through boxing. I also wonder how yet another adult, someone who worked closely with me, didn't see that I was a substance abuser. In retrospect, I can't imagine how I could have worked out so hard and felt so good, physically, then deliberately put poison into my body, basically negating all the work I'd just done.

The next time Mr. Rollins got angry – and it was probably for something I did and should not have – he put his hands up as if to hit me, but this time, I put my hands up as well. I asked him if he wanted to go outside. I felt so empowered being able to defend myself. It was one of the few times in my life up to that point that I was able to control a situation. But, only to a point. While I felt empowered, I also felt that I had crushed something at the same time. By taking a stand, I had altered our relationship, severing something that could never be reconnected. But he never did hit me again.

I've learned in life that even when you gain something, you can lose something else – and vice versa.

All things considered, I am very appreciative of these people who took me out of that institution, into their home, and cared for me. Their impact on my life is why I have raised my children the way I have, why I myself became a foster parent, and ultimately, an adoptive parent. I took their example of seemingly wanting to do good and improved on the expectation and outcome of the results. Positive things so often come from negative situations.

CHAPTER 7

"High" School Days

I did just enough in high school to move on from one grade to the next. I chose how hard I wanted to work at school just to get by. How much was really expected of me, as a 15-year-old African-American kid living in foster care? The world was still a vastly discriminatory place in the late '60's and early 1970's, and virtues like hope and ambition weren't instilled into the psyches of young, black males. On the rare occasion that they were, someone was always around to shoot those aspirations down.

The peaceful Civil Rights rallies rapidly faded after Dr. King's assassination. Instead, the atmosphere of the times, particularly for black Americans, became one of increasing violence.

I watched on television and even witnessed for myself the fires that raged, the looting and devastation that resulted from the racial tensions and social unrest the entire country seemed to be experiencing – many taking place nearly in my own backyard. H Street, NE and Rhode Island Ave, NE were very close to my house on 30th Street, and almost completely wiped out on the night of Martin Luther King's assassination.

The conflict between war and peace, destructive behaviors, confusion and anger and sadness that set the mood for those times was not unlike my own as a high school student, a teenager, an African-American foster child with little guidance, no direction and barely a glimmer of hope for something better.

But, I was a proven survivor. I'd been through my own version of hell, although comparatively speaking, the events of my early childhood probably paled in comparison to the big picture of losses suffered by our country. Dr. King, the Kennedy's, Malcolm X, countless members of the military killed in the war. You can't go through life unscathed by the significant events that shape the time and culture in which you live. How you react and how you allow events to shape and impact your life is probably the best way to gain some kind of control over things which you really can't control.

Between the major local and world issues and the issues of my own personal life, I was, not surprisingly, coming from a place of extreme emotional insecurity. Early in 10th grade, I was still dabbling with drugs, and straddling the fence between being the good guy, but always with the bad guy element. Though I felt like I could be comfortable in any group of peers and I had a lot of friends, there was always, always that underlying feeling that I didn't belong.

Michael and I rode the city bus together to school. He and I were still friends, though not as close as we had once been. He was in the group that you might label the 'nerds," while I was looked at as sort of the cool nerd. I wasn't a full-fledged thug just yet. I was more of a good kid with an edge. Though I hung with the good character kids, because I had that edge, I had the respect of the bad guys, and would use the good guys for my convenience. These are the savvy things I thought I needed to do to get by.

At this point, I was "dating" my first girlfriend, Marie. We were very demonstrative about our feelings, kissing in public and not concerned about what anyone thought. I also spent a lot of time hanging out alone with her, at her house. Looking back on those days now, as the father of five daughters, makes me shudder.

I went to school regularly; I just didn't attend all of my classes so regularly. I would pick and choose the classes I wanted to skip, go to the stairwell and get stoned there with the other "bad kids." The good kids did their best to avoid the stairwell, but I just naturally gravitated toward that place and would hang out, smoke cigarettes, do drugs and shoot craps.

We had the system figured out pretty well, or so we thought. We had our lookouts for teachers and hall monitors, and we knew our escape routes. Things worked out up until almost the end of the school year, when the administration finally figured out a way to catch us by cordoning off the east side of the hall with a gate. When we ran in that direction, we were trapped. Because we were not only cutting class, but caught with drugs and dice, we all got expelled.

Here I was again, removed from a place against my own will. But this time, I had to take responsibility. It was my own doing, my own bad decisions that caused me to get kicked out of school. I couldn't really blame this on anyone else. Sure, the extenuating circumstances of my childhood and upbringing, and the outside influences of peer pressure were factors. But I owned this one.

Because my grades were decent, I was told that I could attend adult evening classes, but at another school. If I caught up in all classes, the principal at McKinley would permit me to return for my final year of high school. So, off I went to Roosevelt High School in NW D.C. – a long, long way from where I lived.

Once again, it was completely up to me to get myself there. For the remainder of that year and the entire 11th grade, I worked my job at McDonald's during the day, and rode the city bus across town at night, alone, to attend classes at Roosevelt, where I was mixed in with students of all ages, including adults. At 15 and 16 years old, I was traveling across town, waiting at bus stops and walking in the dark. The feelings of being alone and lost were becoming all too familiar in my life.

I suppose I could have just not attended those classes. I'd like to think I continued at it, even though it was terribly inconvenient and a bit scary, because I knew I needed to focus on my education. Because I knew that I had to look at more of a long-term plan for my life. Because I knew if I worked hard and kept at it, I would be successful one day. I would like to think that's the reason I took that bus ride to school across town every night for more than a year.

I can't say for certain, but I know that if I hadn't done it, my life would have turned out very differently.

I kept out of trouble as best I could on those night trips to school, but did have a couple of encounters with members of the Nation of Islam, who always tried to talk to me, I guess to recruit me, while I waited for my bus. They were all about raising the spirit, mentality and status of African-Americans, but in 1973, with Malcolm X – the "Voice of the Nation of Islam" in the 1950's and early 1960's – and Dr. King both assassinated, their approach and tactics had become more militant in nature.

I wasn't sure if I was supposed to be afraid or impressed by them; in either case, I didn't get involved. I had plenty of personal injustices in my own life that sparked my anger and resentment, and I suppose I would have been the perfect recruit. Either I was too selfish, focusing on my own trials and tribulations, or I had enough sense to just try to manage the problems that were on my own plate. You can't help others until you first know how to help yourself. It's like those safety instructions they give you on an airplane – secure your own oxygen mask before trying to help others.

In what was supposed to be my senior year, I went back to McKinley to see if I could return to graduate with my class. They allowed me back in, but my curriculum included making up several classes from the 10th grade in addition to my 12th grade classes.

This was probably the best thing that could have happened to me – it is when I had my first encounter with Peaches. Marie and I weren't as close anymore; I was interested in another girl, Sandy, who lived in southeast D.C. Though I saw Peaches at school and was attracted to her, the fact that Sandy lived in southeast made me feel pretty cool. In those days, where you came from was very important. The reality was that whether or not you made it home on any given night depended on where you were. You couldn't just wander into neighborhoods if you didn't belong there. Thugs were very territorial in those days. I guess when you don't have much, you want to protect it with all you've got. You want to feel like you have control over your domain. Me? I felt like I could go anywhere in the city

I would cut school, travel to Sandy's neighborhood and spend the day at her parents' house. We were out of control and did the craziest things. Of course, her parents were at work and didn't know we were there. By this point, I had already explored the fantasies of my early youth with Marie, and was fairly experienced. But Sandy was even more experienced.

I do recall the one time we were very nearly busted by her father when he came home unexpectedly from work. Sandy and I were fooling around in her parents' bedroom, of all places. I hid in the closet while she ran downstairs and made some excuse to her father about why she was home and not in school. She successfully snuck me out of the house, and I'm not sure where I'd be right now if we'd been caught. When I wasn't traveling across town, I was hanging out with the bad guys in my neighborhood. Funny how I keep calling them bad guys, when I was one of them....

We hung out at a park on the main highway on South Dakota Ave., next to the gas station across from Sammy's Liquors. We'd just sit there and smoke and drink for hours, in the evenings and on weekends. Some like-minded neighborhood girls would hang out with us, too. To entertain ourselves, we'd people-watch, as people got on and off the public bus that stopped across the street. One day, Peaches got off that bus.

At that moment, we had been talking about girls and all of our conquests. We focused our conversation on Peaches, and her reputation in the neighborhood. We knew which girls were "active" and which weren't. Peaches was considered a "good" girl. Naturally, being the cool thugs we were, we made a bet as to which one of us would "get" her first. I was on a mission.

The very next day, I saw her when I was walking out of the cleaners. I ran over and introduced myself, but she shot me down. She had heard all about me and had seen the way I acted. Her telling me this just encouraged me to pursue her even harder. I had Sandy, and probably could have had many other girls, but there was something about Peaches. I wish I had been smart enough to change my bad boy ways then and there to win her over. But, maybe my behavior on the outside gave her a glimpse of the kind of guy I really was on the inside. Not everything is what it seems. My existence alone was proof that I was able to overcome major obstacles. Getting the girl was going to be a challenge, but I'd been through a few of those before.

I began approaching her at school, and even mentioned her to one of my foster sisters, who told me they had been friends for years. I begged her to tell Peaches good things about me. One day, she and Peaches came over to my locker. During our conversation, Peaches asked me for some money. I handed it right over. As she walked away, she and her friends started laughing. I'd been "had." She's always been known to be a bit of a prankster.

CHAPTER 8

A Fresh Beginning and a Sour Ending

Though Peaches had routinely rejected all of my attempts to get close to her, by the end of the school year, I did finally convince her to give me her phone number. She was hesitant about me, and rightly so. I was still getting high and hanging out with a bad crowd, and she knew it.

Although I was totally into Peaches at this point, I was still seeing Sandy as well. One day I came clean with Sandy and told her all about Peaches. I'll never forget her words. "That's the girl that's going to take you away from me." I don't know if it was the way I talked about Peaches or Sandy's female intuition, but it was quite a profound statement.

I was so anxious to get back to my own neighborhood to see Peaches after Sandy said that, I actually caught a cab instead of taking the bus. I went straight to the house where Peaches lived with her aunt and uncle, Bessie and Ollie Ward. Peaches' mother had died when she was only 11 years-old, and her aunt and uncle were very protective of her and her sisters.

I was allowed to go by the house to talk with her, but they always pulled her back inside after very brief conversations. I'm not sure whether they knew of my reputation, but their street was along my hang-out route, so they probably had laid eyes on me, at the very least. When they did eventually permit me to enter the house, Peaches and I were only allowed to sit in the front room and talk, with her four-year-old cousin,

Alicia, right between us. Years later, I gave my own daughter, Donna, this very job when her older sister began dating.

I didn't blame the Wards for keeping an eye on me, even back then. They were unsure of who I was and where I was headed. Heck, at that point, I don't think I'd ever been sure of who I was and I certainly had no direction. The one thing I did know, probably from the moment I saw her, was that wherever I was heading, I wanted Peaches to go with me.

On this particular day that Sandy uttered those profound words, I asked Peaches to meet me on the corner before her aunt and uncle could pull her away. I needed to talk with her. I needed her.

She showed up a little while later. I had been sitting on the curb smoking a joint while waiting for her. In my neighborhood, the sight of a young, black male sitting on the curb smoking a joint wasn't especially unusual. I suppose the stereotyping that image conjures up isn't without merit. But, despite the fact that I was a drug user, I wasn't lazy, apathetic and unmotivated. I had a job, and I worked to make sure I got back into high school. I probably could have done a lot more to help myself, but just didn't know how. And I guess I liked the way I felt when I got stoned. A little removed from my feelings.

Peaches wasn't a smoker, but she apparently liked me anyway and listened to me patiently, sensitively and sensibly. With my head buried in my arms, shoulders hunched, sitting there on the curb, I told her that I was afraid.

My foster parents had recently told me I would have to leave their home after I graduated high school. I was 17 years old and would soon age out of the foster care system. I had nowhere to go and no idea what to do.

Peaches reached around and hugged me, stirring feelings inside of me that I'd never before felt. She spoke words that I had never heard from anyone before in my life, telling me that I really was somebody and that she believed in me. In her opinion, I should think about joining the military and making something of myself. One thing about Peaches – then and to this day – once she makes up her mind, she pushes until she persuades you to agree with her decision. It's a quality that has made her a driving force in my life.

She cared about me. For the first time in my life, there was somebody who cared about who I was. Can you even imagine not believing that anyone really cared about you until you were 17? I vowed then and there to work hard at changing. I promised Peaches I would be a different person and stop the drugs and the drinking. I wanted to impress her and get her total approval. We became very close during that short period of time.

I wanted Peaches to go to my prom with me, but her aunt and uncle would not have it. So, I asked Sandy. Maybe it seems odd, but Peaches was okay with it. My foster parents gave me a choice. They would either give me money to rent a car to go to the prom or pay for my graduation. Guess which one that 17-year-old boy chose? (my guess is that *any* 17-year-old boy would have done the same thing. I attended adult evening classes clear across town so that I could get back into my high school, yet I did not walk across the stage with the McKinley High School graduating class of 1976. I did however, drive to the prom in a rented 1976 Cutlass Supreme.

Man, I thought I was just it.

My best friend at the time, Richard Thompson, had asked me to call my old girlfriend Marie to go to the prom with him. So, there I was, in essence, going to the prom with my two old girlfriends while Peaches was at home.

During the prom, Sandy and I got into a crazy argument. I'd had enough and decided it was time to leave. With Marie and Richard in the back seat, Sandy and I screamed at one another while I was driving this cool car. Looking back, maybe I should have opted to walk across that stage with my graduating class. That would have been the better decision and a proud moment for me. I am not at all proud of the memory of prom night.

Sandy kept insisting that I pull over; she wanted to get out of the car. I basically did as she asked and kicked her out of the car. Unfortunately, it wouldn't be the last time I kicked a woman out of my car.

We were on New York Avenue in northeast D.C. Sandy lived all the way southeast, but I pulled over, she got out and walked down the street in her prom gown. And, I drove away. Marie was yelling at me for leaving Sandy, so Richard and I dropped her off and went to the

Landover Mall in Maryland, doing figure 8's in the parking lot for the rest of the night.

I learned later that Sandy ended up making it home okay – she had called her uncle to pick her up. But, the fact is, I left her there without knowing what would happen to her.

CHAPTER 9

The Summer of '76

After the prom, during that summer of '76, I was still doing the usual things I had been doing – hanging out with the guys on my street, partying all over the city, getting rowdy on the buses, and just living a bit on the edge. Although I had promised Peaches I would change, I had made the decision to enlist in the military at this point, and was pretty much willing to do anything, try anything, and get into anything before I had to leave.

The military wasn't simply my best option; it really seemed to be the only choice I had at the time. As soon as I turned 18, I would age out of the foster care system. Meaning, the system would no longer pay the Rollins' a stipend to care for me. As I was approaching that age, my foster parents had made it pretty clear that once I was 18 and that stipend went away, I would have to go, too. That fact had been hammered into my head for quite some time.

Like most soon-to-be high school graduates, I was at a point where I had to figure out what I was going to do next. Joining the U.S. Military wasn't an uncommon option for people in a situation like mine. Then, and to this day. Young people with no means of support – emotional, physical or financial – look to military service as a means to further their education and develop skills.

Even though the military had been desegregated for quite some time, racial divisions were still an issue. But I think I stood a better chance dealing with the racism and prejudice there than I did on the streets of D.C. The Vietnam War had been over for awhile, and joining the military would provide me, as well as other African-Americans, with training and opportunities that we wouldn't have access to otherwise.

Aside from military service, I suppose McDonald's was the one other option that I had. I was still working there, and entertained the idea of attending their university to become a potential manager. For whatever reason, I was good at work. Even though I had all of these negative influences going on in my life, for some reason, I always performed well in my work environment. I cleaned, cooked, and worked the counters. I learned how to cook every item on the McDonald's menu, starting with the breakfasts and then on to the lunches.

My enthusiasm and ability for cooking stemmed from nine years of spending time in the kitchen with Mrs. Rollins. But those nine years were soon coming to a close, and while life with my foster parents was no picnic, I knew full well the army would be no gravy train either.

To this day, I am still conflicted about where I fit in the big picture of the Rollins family. Both are now deceased, but upon attending each one's funeral I was presented as their *foster* son, as were my foster siblings. Even while I was grieving at each one's service, grieving for the person I had allowed myself to consider as mom or dad, their blood family members reminded me that this was yet another place that wasn't really mine. The announcement, the obituary, the program, all identified me as *foster*. I remember thinking at both of their funerals, that at the end of the day, I was a resource for them, not their *son*.

I don't mean to make it sound like the Rollins' just washed their hands of me and didn't care what happened to me one way or the other. That wasn't the case. In fact, before I graduated high school, they did spend an entire day driving around the city with me, looking for a place for me to live. Of course, it had to be a place that I could afford on the income I was making. And, as you might expect, that income wasn't going to land me in a desirable neighborhood. Not even close.

We came across a three-story row house on 1st Street NE, right off New York Avenue, where I could rent a bedroom and have kitchen privileges. I remember looking around and thinking, "This is a scary place." I'd been scared before about the places I'd lived – starting with living at an orphanage. But I had no choice, no control, no voice back then. I knew, at 17 years old, standing in front of those crumbling row houses, with some of the dregs of humanity wandering about, that there was no way I could do this. I was not the cocky thug I pretended to be, the guy who wouldn't be scared of any situation. I think I was beginning to realize I wasn't a thug at all.

As soon as I got home that day, I reached out to Peaches. We talked – about the day, the row houses, McDonald's, the military. I told her how I felt about it all, and by the time we were done, I came to the conclusion that I just couldn't do the row house thing. A decision had to be made, and with Peaches' support and encouragement, I went to the recruiting office that very day. The process was straightforward and simple. As I said, this was a common alternative for African-Americans in the 1970's. The recruiting officers knew exactly what they were doing.

I was scheduled to leave six months later, in February 1977.

I continued working at McDonald's, and decided to take a class at the local university, Federal City College, which is now UDC. Peaches and I were openly dating and getting along very well. I had this gut feeling that this girl was the new inspiration in my life. She gave me insight and reason to live my life on purpose.

As the time for me to actually go into the Army drew nearer, I became more and more nervous and afraid. Afraid to leave home. Afraid to leave Peaches. Afraid of what might happen to me, even though the nation wasn't at war. Who could know for certain when war might break out? And if something did happen, would my family – those people that I knew existed, hadn't seen for years and never forgot about – ever know?

Being part of the foster care system, I had access to my own social worker, so I contacted her to find my siblings – just in case I didn't make it back.

She found Cheryl, Yvette and Olivia. Though we had been virtually strangers all these years, I was so relieved to get to see some of my family again. The girls had all been through foster care, and we shared a lot of pain, both spoken and unspoken, I suppose, as we got reacquainted. Peaches knew my fears, too. She promised me that she would stay faithful. She promised that she would wait for me. At least, in leaving my home this time, I knew I had someone and something to come back to. I knew I would have a home again.

In February of 1977, I took my first ever plane ride - to Oklahoma – and into the U.S. Military.

CHAPTER 10

In the Army

During the initial visit with the local recruiter, the army personnel talked with me about what I wanted to do or be while I was enlisted. This was my opportunity to become all I could be. More accurately, to become all the army wanted me to be.

I told the people at the intake station that I wanted to be a dentist, and believed that the recruiter signed me up for dental training. When I arrived to begin my stint in the army, I was informed that after taking a test and going through a series of questions, I apparently didn't qualify to be a dentist. I was offered an opportunity in Communications. I said okay, again knowing full well that I really had no choice.

I'd heard later on, through conversations with other recruits, that this was standard treatment of minorities in the military. Promotion of black officers was not a priority. This discrimination existed to such a degree that at some point between 1977-1981, Army Secretary Clifford L. Alexander instructed the promotion board to revise a list of proposed promotions because no blacks were on it. On that revised list was Colin Powell, who soared through the military ranks and became chairman of the Joint Chiefs of Staff under President George H.W. Bush. But the direction the army put me in – radio communications – would have a long-standing impact on the rest of my life. Another negative situation that I somehow, eventually, found a way to work to my advantage. If

I could put my finger on it, if there was an actual formula for being positive and persevering, I'd bottle it. Those traits have served me well, but man, they weren't always easy to come by.

Immediately after being told I was assigned to Radio Communications, I boarded a plane at BWI airport heading for Oklahoma. It was a big plane, with stewardesses serving me and everything. I was thinking that, if this is what I'm heading towards, this is the life. That feeling lasted for as long as that first leg of the flight lasted. The next plane was smaller than the first, and the one after that, that landed in Lofton, Oklahoma, was even smaller.

My basic training, in Fort Sill, was a real eye-opener. I'd never been out of the city, other than a couple of road trips with the foster parents back to their origins, and I'd certainly never been anywhere alone. I remember coming off the bus that drove us to the training camp to the screams of someone, whom I quickly came to know as my drill sergeant, telling me to drop and give him twenty. Just a few hours earlier, I had been on a plane with friendly, welcoming stewardesses….. I was totally shaken – actually, I was scared to death. I didn't even know what he meant by "give me twenty." When I saw the other guys around me dropping to the ground and doing push-ups, I really panicked. Before that day, I don't think I'd ever done a push-up in my life. Nevertheless, push-ups and constantly being hollered at became a way of life for me for the next six to eight weeks.

There were big, strong-looking guys going through all of this right alongside me. All the while I was thinking that they could handle it while I was just scared, little Dennis. I did everything the drill sergeant told me to do, yet so many of these big and bad guys were just falling apart. I remember some of them crying, trying to find ways to leave. They were even calling their moms to see how they could get signed out.

I remember thinking how odd it was that I somehow had the ability to get through all of this, relatively unscathed. I suspect that the years I unwillingly served in the orphanage prepared me well for this life of discipline and subservient behavior.

After basic training, I went into advanced training and learned about radio communications. Typical of me, I did okay; just enough to get by. Being in the military still didn't feel completely real to me.

I felt like I was walking around in a daze most of the time; like being in a dream.

I stayed in touch with Peaches regularly, saving up my quarters so I could call her on the pay phone, hoping that I would reach her at home. It was a lot more difficult to connect with people back in the days before cell phones. Back then, you really had a 50-50 chance of actually talking with the person you were trying to call; today, you just keep dialing and texting all their different numbers until you track them down.

When I couldn't reach Peaches, I'd call Mr. or Mrs. Rollins, just to hear a friendly, familiar voice and have some connection to people from home. We'd send letters back and forth, too. I still have the letters and pictures people sent to me while I was in the army, some of which carried the scent of Peaches' perfume.

After a few months at Fort Sill, I got transferred to my permanent duty station at Fort Riley, Kansas. I was in the 1st Infantry Division, 49th Ordinance, and a member of the radio communications squadron. I bunked with two other guys in a coed dorm in Fort Riley, which looked very much like a college campus dorm. The similarity ended there.

The army routine was a lot more structured and much stricter than college life, though. We got up early, made our beds, did some physical training before breakfast, and then went to chow. I have to say, the food was always very good and so were all of the facilities.

After breakfast, we'd go to work, like everybody else. Our jobs were to train and prepare for any type of incident or situation that would call us to military activity. That was my everyday life for quite some time. Once we settled in, we were allowed to go into Junction City, Kansas, a town right outside the military base. As you'd expect from a group of 18 year olds, in our free time, we'd go into town as a group and hang out at the clubs or go to parties. One of the guys invited me to go to church with him in Junction City. Of course, he made the invitation much more enticing by telling me all about the girls who also went to church there. Yes, I was still with Peaches, but she was back home and I was 18, so here I was going to church to meet girls – again.

I ended up joining the church choir, and also took up karate. I was in the Tenors, as usual, and the choir, as in the past, was a goldmine for where the girls were.

One of the girls seemed to be as interested in me as I was in her. What I didn't know at the time was that most of the girls in Junction City were positioning themselves to capture a guy that was in the military.

This particular girl had been married before, also to a military guy, and was divorced with two children. I met her whole family – mother, father, brothers and sisters – and I got pretty close with her brother, who was an accomplished boxer in the area – and very popular. We hit it off right from the start, and then I found out that he was a drug dealer. Basically, very quickly after that, I was back into dealing drugs. A familiar pattern for me – meet a popular guy, find out he's into drugs, get caught up, start dealing. I was just this guy's most recent connection to the base, not the chosen one I made myself out to be in my mind. I dealt for about a year.

This time though, the drug was cocaine, not marijuana. I began dealing to other soldiers which was really nothing new on the military base. Drug use in the military gained recognition and notoriety during the Vietnam War, but it was prevalent in soldiers well before then. On breaks from training, I usually drove the Ford LTD all the way back home to visit Peaches. I was also still seeing the girl from Junction City and meeting other girls through the church. I continued to keep up my tennis skills and ended up getting pretty close with another tennis player and military person, who was of course, female. She was in the National Guard and lived in Topeka.

I added Topeka to my list of driving destinations, visiting this girl on the weekends. We both joined the United States Tennis Association (USTA) and participated in actual tournaments on the local tennis circuit. I even got a USTA ranking.

Life seemed pretty good to me at the time. I was playing tennis, still messing around with drugs and had girlfriends all over the place. In retrospect, it was a lot like my high school years, except for the fact that I was in the military. I was young and strong and feeling on top of the world. But, in reality, I was still out of control. The army can teach you discipline, it can teach you honor, it can teach you to protect, it can teach you a skill. But it can't teach you many of the things that should be instilled in a young person from birth – a value and respect for family and self. I would never be able to manage my life properly until I learned those things.

I did maintain my drive and ambition – and my anger. A platoon mate and I were both jockeying for the leadership position of our squadron. When I want something, I want it bad, and went full out to be chosen, but wasn't. I lashed out verbally at the soldier who was, refused to cooperate and eventually we ended up in a fight. I lost my temper, just as I had way back when I was in that classroom at the orphanage. In both instances, my anger stemmed from my desire to achieve, my inability to control the outcome and my insecurities over that lack of control.

Although I was disciplined by the Army unit commander, the incident was never marked on my permanent record.

I had quite a few soldier friends; we were all around the same age and shared similar and varied interests. Collecting albums was very popular and we were all into that. Some of the guys joined other churches and became, in my opinion, fanatics – giving up their worldly goods and possessions. One guy claimed he was born again and started giving away all his albums. We got into a huge debate about religious beliefs out in the courtyard in front of a big group of people. I challenged him and asked questions about why any God would allow people to starve, fight wars and be victims of violence. I thought I was so cool, taking on this zealot and shutting him down with my words. Everyone started calling me *preacher* after that. In my youthful wisdom, I thought I had done something big.

The older I get, the more I know now that shooting down other people's beliefs and ideologies only comes from a person's own insecurities. There's no harm in finding something to believe in that makes you feel positive and doesn't adversely affect other people,

I believed in Peaches. Her presence was always, always with me while I was in the military. Her name was never far from my mind or my lips, even while I was involved with other women. They often told me, just as Sandy had many years earlier, that she would always be the one.

Though Peaches and I communicated constantly, I didn't communicate everything, never telling her about any of my interactions with other girls. She told me she was being faithful, but since I never actually said that I was, I felt I wasn't really lying. Of course, it was a lie by omission. I was 18, I was alone, in the military, and other women wanted me. Was I being a player? Was I insecure that if Peaches found out, I'd lose her? Probably both.

Soon though, Peaches and I began talking about marriage. We'd been boyfriend and girlfriend for quite some time. It felt natural, it felt right, and so the planning began.

My foster parents and Peaches' aunt and uncle helped with all of the planning. I had little to do with anything. I was finally going to be with the woman I knew I was meant to be with, yet the whole time my wedding was being planned, I was still running around, partying and seeing other girls. My foster parents would call me and update me on the plans as they were being made. For my part, I told them how to get in touch with the guys who I wanted to be part of the wedding party. We had nine bridesmaids and nine groomsmen in our wedding party.

I still clearly remember telling the girl I had been seeing in Topeka that I was getting married. We were at her parents' house for a barbecue; I took her out front, sat her on the steps and told her that I really cared about her, but I had this girl back home and that she'd been waiting for me. We both started crying, I felt terrible about hurting this girl's feelings, but I told her that I really had to go back home, there was just something about Peaches. It was a really tough moment, but we managed to get through it.

Heartbreak and overcoming obstacles and pain are part of life.

CHAPTER 11

TYING THE KNOT

I got leave and flew back home for my wedding. It was a huge affair, with all those bridesmaids and groomsmen. We were to be married at the Isle of Patmos Baptist Church in NE D.C. on August 25, 1979.

The night before we got married, I sat down with Peaches at my foster parents' home and told her about all of the girls I'd been involved with while she and I were together. Maybe it was a little crazy of me, but it turned out to be exactly the right thing to do. I needed to let her know everything, up front, before we said our vows. I was 21 years old and felt like I'd been through it all, and I was done with it. I promised that it would be her, and only her, for the rest of my life. Looking back on it now, I'm not sure if I really understood and meant what I was saying, but Peaches accepted and believed it.

In retrospect, that was probably one of the biggest risks I've ever taken. Bigger even than dealing drugs. Sure, that could have landed me in prison, but eventually I'd have gotten out. Losing Peaches would have been a life sentence. And believe me, I fully appreciate the risk that she took as well, by having faith in my commitment to her.

Our wedding reception was held at Peaches' aunt and uncle's home. About midway through the evening, one of my friends spilled a glass of wine all over my outfit, which upset me quite a bit. I grabbed Peaches and we decided to leave early and get started on our honeymoon. We drove off in my car, a 5-speed green Chevy Vega hatchback. That car burned so much oil I had to keep a case of it in the trunk at all times to keep it running.

We headed toward Kings Dominion, VA, but only got as far as Quantico before the muffler fell right out of the Vega. I tied it up with a hanger, but knew the car wasn't going to make the rest of the trip. In my pocket was the money we received from friends and relatives as wedding gifts – about $200-$300. That was all I had on me. We got off the highway and drove into the city, going from hotel to hotel in downtown D.C. asking if we could rent a honeymoon suite. As the desk clerks told us the price, we realized we didn't have enough money for that type of luxury, so we drove back to New York Avenue, not two blocks away from Peaches' aunt and uncle's house, and stayed in a motel that night. It was all we could afford.

But we were together, we were married, and it was our honeymoon night. That was all that really mattered.

We stayed at Peaches' family's home for the next couple of days before I had to go back to the base. Peaches flew out for a visit a couple of months later; it was her first ever time flying. We shared a wonderful week together, living at the home of one of my buddies while he and his wife were on vacation.

I was down to six months on my three-year military term, so it wouldn't be long before we could live together and have a normal marriage. I couldn't wait to have a real home with my bride. After all the years of being "placed" into living situations, I would finally, finally get to choose.

CHAPTER 12

UNEXPECTED INSPIRATION

A little while before my discharge from Fort Riley, I started to really think about what I'd do with my life once I was a civilian again. To be honest, I was nervous about what life would be like outside of the military. I'd grown accustomed to the discipline and the routine, to knowing each day exactly what I would be doing. Now, I had no idea what I'd do once I was on my own.

As excited as I was to be discharged and start my life with Peaches, I knew that I only had a few short months to figure out how to do that.

One afternoon a couple of friends and I were walking around Junction City, just killing some time. We started browsing in a bookstore, not looking for anything in particular, when I saw something there that I'd never seen before. And I'm not exaggerating when I say that it changed my life.

I found a copy of *Black Enterprise Magazine*. It was the most amazing thing I'd ever seen. For the first time in my 21 years, I saw African-Americans portrayed in such a positive light. Suddenly, I felt a glimmer of hope begin to run through me.

I bought that magazine, and devoured very page, every word. I was amazed by what I was reading, about African-Americans who were successful business people, who had set goals and achieved them. Those stories set me alight. I read about people who had risen above troubled beginnings, and not just because they were lucky or because someone else made it happen. These people took charge of their lives. They made decisions. They succeeded.

Until that time, I'd really only made two positive decisions – to enlist, and to marry Peaches. But now I was inspired. I still wasn't sure what I would do when I got home, but I knew it would be a far cry from the life I'd led.

As soon as I finished that first copy, I mailed in the subscription form and waited anxiously for the next issue to arrive. I was so impressed by the magazine that after reading three or four issues, I wrote a letter to the founder, Earl Graves. Maybe it was a crazy thing to do, but I explained my situation to him, and asked for advice about what to do with my life.

Since I wasn't sure how long it would take to get a response, if I got one at all, I used my foster parents' address as the return address on that letter. About four months later I received a reply from Earl Graves' brother, who was an executive editor of *Black Enterprise.* He offered some general advice, telling me to pursue an education and work hard, but nothing really specific or personal.

Nevertheless, I was still inspired by the magazine, and very grateful to have gotten any reply at all. It changed something inside of me and I made up my mind that one day *I* would be profiled in *Black Enterprise.*

My attitude about the future wasn't the only thing that changed when I got home from service. My relationship with my foster parents was different, too. We had communicated fairly regularly while I was away, but by the time I came home and was setting up my life as an adult, with my wife, we talked only about once a month. I was becoming very independent, in part because of the "you're on your own" type of feeling that the army had instilled in me.

But that wasn't the only reason. I was finding my own way and felt I didn't need my foster parents anymore. They had drawn that line of separation when I was 18, making it clear that I would be on my own from then on. I was still feeling bitter about that, so I drew the line too. If they felt that they no longer needed to take care of me, I'd show them that I didn't need their care anyway.

CHAPTER 13

A New Beginning

After my discharge from the Army in February 1980, Peaches and I moved into her family's home. This wasn't exactly how I wanted my new independent life to begin, and I was more than a little uncomfortable about the living arrangement. I'd always had the feeling that her aunt and uncle hadn't been too keen on her being involved with me at the beginning. I assumed they knew my reputation, but they really didn't know anything else about me.

They did, however, host and pay for our wedding, so I guess they had warmed up to me by then, and welcomed us into their home.

It can't be easy to invite someone to live in your home. And it isn't easy being the person moving into someone else's home, either. On that point, I think I can claim to be the expert. I learned this more than once, moving into an orphanage, a foster home and then a military home. Personal routines and habits often need to be adjusted to fit the needs of the many. There's a learning curve involved – for everyone. While it was frustrating for me to not be completely on my own, I was moving into a true home, with a true family – people who cared for and about *me* – Dennis Harris, the individual. A far cry from any of the "homes" I'd previously lived in.

For awhile, I felt that Aunt Bessie and Uncle Ollie were way too involved in my relationship with Peaches. Insecurity can really do a number on a person's perspective. These people may have been Peaches' aunt and uncle, but they were more like parents to her – she'd lived with them since she was very young. They treated her the way parents would treat their children. But, at the time, I was almost fighting to take my place in my relationship with Peaches, and wanted to let them know I had things under control. I suppose I may have had the underlying fear of the bottom dropping out and losing this whole family, too. So instead, I asserted myself and set out to prove that I could take care of Peaches and myself.

On a trip to a family event in Aunt Bessie and Uncle Ollie's hometown in Virginia, Aunt Bessie and I got into an argument. I'm not clear on the cause, but my guess that I probably had a chip on my shoulder. I always did back then. Our relationship made me feel awkward. Sometimes they introduced me as "son-in-law," and other times as "nephew-in-law" When you're born with one name, grow up with another and have been searching for your place and your identity for as long as I had, something like this becomes a major issue.

I vividly recall pulling over and telling Aunt Bessie to get out of the car. In some ways, I hadn't progressed very far from that high school kid who left Sandy on the street in downtown D.C. on prom night. But, I had something at this moment that I didn't have back then. Peaches. She convinced me to let Aunt Bessie back in. After she got back into the car, Aunt Bessie told me that she loved both my wife *and* me, but I was belligerent. I thought she only cared about me because of Peaches.

All I knew for sure was that I wanted to be a man who could provide a home for his wife. I told myself that we wouldn't live with her family for more than a month.

That meant I needed to find a job. . I looked every day, all over the D.C. area, but didn't have any luck.

Then I learned about a company in Silver Springs, MD, that was hiring. I took a bus out there the very next day, completed an application, had an interview, and was offered a job on the spot.

The company, Rixon, manufactured modems, and I was hired as a level-one test technician, based on my military experience in radio repair. I started work the following week, taking that long bus ride every day. Not only did the training and education I received in the military pay off – my starting salary was $6.23 per hour – not bad for 1980 –

but so did the life lessons of patience and perseverance I accumulated during those long bus rides to continuing education classes after being thrown out of high school.

Peaches had been working since high school in the pharmacy department at Memco Department Store, and made about the same amount of money I did. We were anxious to get our own place, and with both of us working and saving, she found an apartment for us within a month.

Our first real home. It was a one-bedroom in the Dodge Park Apartments in Prince Georges County, MD. It wasn't an ideal location, but it was ours. The neighborhood was nicknamed "Dodge City" because there were shootings almost every night.

Some things, like drugs, crime and gangs, transcend generations, but I had seen enough in my 21 years to know that lifestyle wasn't for me. I could have easily continued down that path toward becoming a total thug once I was out of high school. But something drove me, something guided me, something willed me to push forward when it would have been easier to fall back. What was it that kept me on the right track? I wanted better for me and I wanted better for my family, when I finally did have one. It wasn't easy to trade the safety we felt in Peaches' aunt and uncle's home for the not-so-safe privacy of our own place, but Peaches and I decided to stay focused on one another, mind our own business, and not get caught up in what happened on the street.

We were on our way. I recall that the movie "Fame" was out then, and that song was all over the radio. I used to hear it in my head as I rode to work – "Look at me and tell me what you see. You ain't seen the best of me yet. Give me time I'll make you forget the rest." That's how I felt as Peaches and I were finally getting started on our life. We'd build such a good future that the bad times of the past would be forgotten.

We worked hard, concentrating on our own lives and trying to ignore what went on in the neighborhood. Before too long, Peaches was pregnant, and within a year of moving into our place, our first child was born.

I can honestly say that my daughter's birth is still one of the most profoundly moving experiences of my life. Seeing my wife endure such pain in order to bring this child into the world was overwhelming. I'd never seen a truer expression of love than what she went through that day, and I vowed then and there that I would be with her forever.

I was a father. I had a family. My most desperate wish, yearned for dream, aching need finally realized. The birth of my child was the most meaningful moment in my life and I knew that, no matter what, I would always be a meaningful part of her life.

We saw Aunt Bessie and Uncle Ollie often, particularly after Desiree was born, since they lived close by our first home. Uncle Ollie was usually in the kitchen with other male relatives, talking about business, work, politics, or church. I began to listen in on these conversations, and for the first time in my life, I realized that staring me right in the face was the image of what a father should be. I listened to their wisdom and experiences, and I looked forward to going over there. Though none of them had their own businesses at the time, they became like mentors to me.

Peaches' uncle and I decided to look into purchasing property through a program with the Department of Housing and Urban Development. At the same time, one of my sisters had inherited money from insurance when her husband died, and reached out to me for advice. I suggested that she allow me to invest her money in a property that Uncle Ollie and I wanted to purchase. Peaches and I became partners with Aunt Bessie and Uncle Ollie in a four-unit apartment building.

I was starting to see Uncle Ollie as the father I never had. We played "good cop, bad cop" when it came to tenants. I was the bad cop. Uncle Ollie would work out payments with the tenants and would call me in if they needed to be evicted.

We sold the property for a nice profit after about six years. The biggest profit of all, though, was how close our family became.

We enjoy each other's company to this day, whenever we're together. I don't think a "real mother and father" could have been closer to me than my in-laws. I don't ever take them for granted.

CHAPTER 14

SPIRITUAL AWAKENING

Throughout my relationship with Peaches, and even with all the joy that Desiree brought to our lives, I found myself having moments of what I suppose was depression. Every few months, they would hit me out of nowhere, for no apparent reason.

I'd begin to feel lost and would become very self-absorbed and reflective, withdrawing into myself. During these periods, I talked a lot about my childhood and my time in foster care.

Peaches was always there to listen. She was incredible through all of it. Here she was taking care of a newborn, keeping house, and dealing with my moods. I don't know how she did it. And I don't know how I would have made it without her.

So many significant and insignificant things happen throughout the course of a person's life, and even though the years may go by, those random moments tend to resurface without warning. That's the case for anyone, I suppose. And as much as we would like to suppress those memories and events that are unpleasant, rarely are we able to do so.

Peaches knew me well enough to know that, now that I was a parent, all those feelings about being left by my own mother were beginning to resurface. She suggested that maybe it was time to look for my mother.

I started to look through the telephone book for names that matched my birth certificate, randomly dialing numbers, awkwardly asking women if they were my mother. Boy, did I get some reactions to those calls! Some people wanted to help me, some hung up, some cursed at me.

I'd do this for awhile, then stop and get back to my regular routine, until the feelings hit me again and I'd start all over.

Peaches and I both continued working hard and started thinking about our future, and I became fixated on buying a house. We spoke to a real estate agent, and were prequalified for a mortgage of under $50,000.00. It's funny to think now about how low that amount is for a house, but back then, we were scared to death at the thought of borrowing that much money.

We found a house in Landover, MD. It was small – 600 square feet – but it was ours. It was a safe place to raise our daughter, and to build a happy home. And it was much closer to my job, which was definitely a plus.

Although I didn't have that long daily commute, I'd used those many, many hours of traveling to do a lot of thinking – about myself, my family, and our future. I took my responsibilities as a husband and now, a father, very seriously. I was fully committed to building the best possible life for my family. Despite any uncertainties I had about myself, there was one thing I knew to be an indisputable fact – no child of mine would ever endure the things I'd lived through.

With all this on my mind, I wanted to start advancing at work. The engineers and a lot of the techs at Rixon had degrees, and I knew that was the way to go if I wanted to get ahead. I enrolled in Prince Georges Community College, taking classes at night toward a degree in electronic engineering.

And life went on. Three years after Desiree's birth, in 1982, our daughter Dorian was born. There's a kind of funny story about how we chose her name. I'd been working nights for awhile and taking classes during the day, and somehow I got started watching the soap opera *One Life to Live* in the afternoons. There was a character I liked, a woman named Dorian Lord, whose tenacity I admired. I guess I admired it so much that I suggested we give our daughter that name, hoping she'd have the same quality. I'm still sort of surprised that Peaches went along with the idea.

At this point in my life, I was elated! Now we felt even more like a family – two children, a house, a good job. Billy Joel had a song out at the time, "She's Got a Way." I used to think about how, of course, I felt that way about my wife, but now I had our two girls as well, and did they ever have a way to move me. Sometimes I was overcome by just how much love I felt for those three ladies.

And one thing I'll say for my ladies, they were truly my inspiration to succeed. By the time I received my degree, I had four or five years experience under my belt at Rixon, and I was promoted to Test Technician III. I was glad for the promotion, of course, but with my determination to make the best life possible for my family, I started thinking about the career path that lay ahead of me.

One day something happened at work that really focused my thinking about the future. I received a statement of the company's retirement plan. It said that I'd be eligible to retire in 2026, at which time I would receive $600 a month in pension.

That was a real "light bulb moment." I knew that there was no way I was going to work my entire life for *$600 a month*. I found that entirely unacceptable, even depressing. Right then and there, I decided to take control of my life and figure out a way to do something that would change that expectation. I wanted so much more than that for my family.

Like a lot of people in the early 80's, I looked into working for Amway, figuring I could make decent money by selling their products. I got all the information and the starter kit, but it just sat on my dresser. I never pursued it.

But it wasn't a waste of time, because something did come out of it. I started to think like an entrepreneur. I knew I had the right spirit, now all I needed was an idea.

During this time, Rixon was bought by a multi-million dollar conglomerate called Schlumberger. This was around 1984, when AT&T was divested and corporations began to buy their own telecommunications exchanges and private branch exchanges, or PBXs, and set up their own internal systems. When my company decided to form a telecommunications department, a lot of people applied for the new jobs, from both inside and outside the company. I applied right away, and was offered a position as a telephone technician.

The new department manager told me that my resume was the only one that included any telecommunications experience. I had my time in the military to thank for that. When I was in the army, we did field exercises where we'd throw telephone wire up into the trees, trying to connect the officers' tents back to a switchboard so that they could communicate with one another. It was this experience with running wire that got me the new job.

The manager and I were the first two employees in the new department. Our first assignment was to completely wire the entire building to connect the new PBX. Fortunately for me, my boss asked me to work with Northern Telecom Systems, the company that manufactured the PBX, to get the building set up. Working with the Northern technicians, I figured out how to program telephone features and lines throughout the building. When they turned over the system to us, the company sent me for more training at Northern so that I could take over managing the system.

As I was getting involved with my new job, something very dynamic was also going on in my personal life. Peaches' youngest sister was dating the brother of one of my high school friends, who was a member of Pleasant Lane Baptist Church. Whenever he and my sister-in-law came to visit, he talked a lot about the church.

Although he was much younger than Peaches and I, he was very involved with the church, and eventually convinced us to attend a service. We finally went one Sunday morning, and were both absolutely amazed by the preacher's presentation. We came away with a new perspective. After just a few visits, we decided to join the church.

That decision impacted my life in so many ways. It's kind of hard to believe, but almost immediately, the church decided that I had leadership potential. Maybe my old army buddies who'd called me Preacher had seen something in me that I didn't realize was there.

I don't even think we were members for two months before the pastor asked me to take charge of the renovation of a church-owned property next door to the main sanctuary. I was impressed by the request – maybe overly impressed – and Peaches and I jumped in, full speed. After all, I was only 27, and here I was being asked to take a leadership role.

We became almost fanatics about the church, and I started raising my hand whenever they asked for help with anything. I spent every spare moment at the church. Right after work, early mornings, on weekends, late at night – I was totally focused on the renovation of the Fellowship Hall.

It took about eight months to complete the renovation. The church and the members were very impressed that I'd gotten it done so well, and the place was so nice that they nominated me to become a member of the Board of Trustees.

There was an official meeting where the pastor called for nominations and someone proposed my name. This was still during my first year as a member of the church. What's more, at that same meeting, they voted to make me the chairman of the board of trustees. Talk about up-and-coming! I was probably in over my head, but I was too caught up in the excitement to realize it.

Now I was part of the church leadership. And within the next year, there was talk of me becoming a deacon. It was amazing to think of how quickly things were happening in the church. I felt that I'd finally found my place.

On November 25, 1984, just a few months after the birth of Dorian, Peaches and I were ordained as deacons of PLBC. And just months later, I was voted in as vice-chairman of the deacon board. I was now third in leadership of the church. Plus, I was named chairman of the department of finance and revenue, which meant that I handled the church's money.

In the meantime, I was still working hard at my job. When the company wanted to have the same telecommunications system throughout all its locations, I began flying to different offices to upgrade their systems. Back at the main office, I started to inventory and unpack systems and handle storage, and became interested in figuring out how to get smaller systems to work and connect to big PBX systems.

I worked on this on my own time, during lunch hours, at night and on weekends – or, when I wasn't at the church. One day I got it to work, running from one end of the building to the other, patching in a call. I ran to my boss's office to tell him, and ended up having another light bulb moment. My boss was excited about it, and I felt he was proud of me. Because I'd thought of him as a mentor, his positive reaction meant a lot.

If he was proud, he was certainly the only one. My coworkers resented me working on my own time – I hadn't charged the company any overtime for the extra hours I'd worked, and they felt I was making them look bad.

I wasn't worried about what my coworkers thought because our goals weren't the same. I was not content to bring home my paycheck and wait for that $600 a month retirement plan. I was on a different mission now.

CHAPTER 15

Striking Out On My Own

Throughout this time, while I was learning more and more at work and was so heavily involved with the church, the idea of starting my own business was also in and out of my mind. Based on my positive experience with PLBC, I began to feel that I could lead, that I could do anything. My success in leading the congregation, combined with the new knowledge I'd gained at work, made me begin to feel confident that I could start my own business.

In 1986, I decided to try to branch out on my own. I named my new business Telecommunications Services Company, TSC. I had business cards and flyers printed, bought a set of tools, and pretty much operated out of the trunk of my car. I figured I'd be a telephone technician for individuals or small companies, doing the same type of work that I did in my full-time job.

Looking back, I really started that company with no business background or even any real understanding of how to run a business. I'd always been a big reader, but around this time, just when our third child, Donna, was born, I gave up novels for business books. I also enrolled in the community college, taking classes like sales and marketing, things that would help with business development. With three children now, I knew that I couldn't mess around. I needed to make my business work.

Things changed in 1987, Rixon had a lay-off and the entire telecommunications department was let go. My thoughts went immediately to working full-time on my own company. I kicked into gear, trying to figure out how to make my occasional, part-time installation business into something bigger that would support my family.

Fortunately, I had participated in the 401k plan and was also given six weeks severance pay. I told Peaches that I wanted to try to make a go of my own company, but thought that I needed more money to do it. As she always had, she believed in my commitment to this plan and in my determination to make it work. We decided to take a leap of faith. I cashed in the 401k, which was worth about $10,000, opened a business checking account, and bought a computer. That computer cost $2,000. It was the main investment, the anchor of the business. And in 1987, computers weren't the sleek little laptops we use today. They were big and bulky, very expensive, and very slow – although it was still faster than anything else I'd ever seen at the time.

I took a little section of the second bedroom, set up the computer on a small table, and called it my home office. With the computer and printer, I started developing and printing brochures.

With no customers yet, I started going around in parking lots with Desiree, who was about five years old, putting flyers on car windshields. I got some calls for residential work, for jobs like installing a new telephone jack in someone's home, earning $25 or $30 for a job. This led to working for a few home-based businesses, too.

I realized quickly that I didn't want to stay with residential work. I disliked messing with people's homes, tearing up their walls (either on purpose or accidentally). It just wasn't for me. I wanted to work for businesses. That seemed like a more professional, steady type of work that I thought I'd enjoy.

I got a list of local companies at the library and put my business plan to work. Back in those early days, my business model was basically to just send out fliers to all these companies, offering my services. I mailed out a couple hundred, and given how rudimentary it was, felt fortunate that I actually got some responses.

Within months of going full-time with my business, Rixon called with an offer. They asked if I'd take care of the phone system that

I'd been trained on, since they no longer had a telecommunications department. I'd made sure that they knew I was starting my own business when I was laid off, and since they'd had me trained and knew I was certified in their telecom systems, they felt comfortable asking me to handle the work.

Of course, I accepted the offer. Now I was making more as a contractor to them than I'd been making when I was on their payroll. Two thousand dollars a month! It seemed like a really big deal at the time, although today as a businessman, I realize that of course I'd charge them more than I'd earned as an hourly employee. But then I was thrilled; I felt that they'd recognized something positive about me. And recognition was still something I needed. The best part was that I could dial in remotely from my computer and program things back at the company. I only had to go there once or twice a week, which left me time to work on my own business.

Now that I had my first real contract, I knew that I had to get out of that little bedroom space. I moved into my first office – just one room – but now my company was really up and running.

That contract was the anchor to building my company, and it gave me the confidence to move forward. I was invited to bid on a contract to run cable in the buildings of a local utility. I won the contract, although without fully understanding how these things worked, I bid it to win it, but not to really make any money. It was a lesson learned early.

CHAPTER 16

Disillusionment and Depression

As my business was growing, I was still extremely involved with PLBC, the place where I had gained the confidence and strength to venture out on my own. Whenever the church needed money, we started a building fund program. As a deacon and chairman of finance, I spoke at those programs to try to raise money. I appealed to the congregation with such emotion and inspiration that people would give up all the money they had. Probably 80 percent of the congregation lived on fixed incomes, and they were giving up their hard-earned rent money because of my appeals.

I would stand in front of the congregation and write a check, then hold it up and tell the people that this was my wife's and my sacrifice for the church. I vividly recall the members following me, although in retrospect I see it more like leading sheep to the slaughter. But at the time, I was very sincere in my tear-jerking appeals. I broke every record for fund-raising, every time. In my tenure, the church raised more money than in all of its previous history.

In addition to the fund-raising appeals, as deacon I was required to take turns preaching. We deacons delivered "sermonettes," which were not full sermons and were not delivered from the pulpit. In fact, the pastor wouldn't allow us to preach from the pulpit, nor were we supposed to generate as much enthusiasm as he did. I wonder why he even let us preach at all, since he apparently wanted all the recognition to himself. But that didn't matter to me at the time. I'd spend weeks working on my sermonettes, writing and practicing until I got a similar reaction to the minister's.

During this time, the dynamic between the pastor and me began to change. It seems that I had unintentionally developed a following within the church, and without my knowledge, they told the pastor that they wanted to hear me speak more often, whether in fund-raising or sermonettes.

Frankly, the pastor had issues with this, and wasn't too happy about my increasing popularity. That became clear when I sat with him and described my ambitions for starting my company. He tried to discourage me, saying that starting the company would only serve me and not be of any benefit to anyone else. I've never forgotten that, because it seems to fly in the face of everything I believed a pastor should do for his congregation.

I still felt very fanatical and devoted to my church and religious experience, but I was beginning to feel an animosity between me and the pastor. I was torn, and was growing increasingly uncomfortable.

What added fuel to the fire was that I had begun to spend more time on my business than I did at the church. The church had been accustomed to seeing me every time the doors were open. In fact, I was the one who opened the doors. And now I'd found another priority, one that PLBC didn't see as a benefit.

I was involved in winning contracts to build my company. I would be late to bible study and the deacon meetings, and now was being chastised for it. Basically, I was told to choose between the church and my business. I struggled with this for a long time, not at all sure of what I should do.

I kept going to church, but ultimately reached the point where I'd feel physically sick on Sunday morning once I got there. When the pastor started preaching, I found that I couldn't even listen to him – I'd get very anxious and feel panicked, and would end up leaving in the middle of the service, going downstairs to the rest room until it was over.

Eventually, I stopped going at all. Given how deeply committed I'd been to the church, this represented a huge change in my life. It was as if something had been removed from my soul, as if some essential part of me was gone. I didn't know how to handle the loss.

One Sunday morning the church sent the chairman of the deacon board to my house to check on me. As we sat in the living room, I tried to explain what was going on, but the more I tried to tell him how I felt, the more upset I became.

He told me, "It's not the church; it's you," and he actually asked me if I was having an affair. I can't even describe how stunned I was by that, although I shouldn't have been surprised. I knew from my experience as vice-chairman that whenever anyone had a problem with the church, the pattern was to always blame the person. The church was never at fault.

In my case, over the previous six months I'd begun to verbalize my feelings about the church's reaction to people's concerns. So I knew full well that I'd be blamed if I said I felt uncomfortable with some of the things that were happening at the church.

For example, the pastor had asked my wife and me to co-sign a car loan for him, which we did. He bought a Cadillac, and of course, didn't keep up with the payments. Every time he missed a payment, we'd get a call for the money. I also realized that he was using some of the money from the fund-raisers for personal reasons. I felt betrayed when I saw that all of the congregation's hard-earned money wasn't going to the church. I knew he was preaching one thing but his character didn't back it up.

And when I tried to explain all of this to the vice-chairman, he asked me if I was having an affair.

That reaction took me over the edge. I'm not exaggerating when I say that I ended up having a nervous breakdown. Right there, at that moment, trying to explain my feelings to the chairman of the deacon board.

In that instant, I went into a time of depression that I thought would never end.

I was in bad shape, so bad that Peaches insisted I see a doctor. I was diagnosed as clinically depressed, put on medication and made to go to therapy.

Here I was, trying to run a business, trying to figure out my spiritual life, and now I also had a regular weekly therapy appointment that I wasn't even sure was helping me at all. I wasn't sleeping at night and didn't want to get up in the morning. All I wanted was to be in a dark room, hiding under the covers.

Even the thought of my daughters wasn't enough to make me want to face the day. I felt so lost inside of myself that I didn't think I could face their beautiful smiles and happy laughter. I was their father. I was the person devoted to giving them everything they needed, but I felt that I had nothing left. If I couldn't fix myself, if I couldn't make myself happy, how could I possibly take care of them?

At the point where I believed I couldn't take it any longer, I woke up one night with an overwhelming feeling of dread. I decided that I would kill myself. It seemed to be the only solution, the best thing to do. Everything just felt like too much for me to bear. The world was a dark and lonely place again, and again, I didn't know where I belonged. Just like when I was a young child, here I was trying to understand and trying to belong, and not finding any answers.

As depressed as I was, I suppose that I knew deep down that I couldn't commit suicide. Instead of just doing it, I told Peaches how I felt. Needless to say, I scared the life out of her, but once again, her strength and devotion saved me. She took the day off and stayed with me. I was afraid to leave the house, consumed by anxiety and fear. For days, Peaches had to go with me wherever I went.

The therapist gave me tools that helped me through moments of panic, and the treatment did help. But that period sent me back to my early life, to the times when I'd had such low self-esteem. It's ironic that after my church leadership experience, which helped to build my confidence and enable me to start my business, my self-esteem now reverted back to those early days.

I honestly believe that, to this day, I still haven't fully recaptured it. Each day I have to prepare myself for the world, gather enough self-esteem to get through the day. That period of deep depression was a very damaging time for me.

But if there can be a positive aspect to that time, I believe it's this – when I look back at that terrible period of my life and what it took to get through it, the things I have ultimately achieved feel even greater, the accomplishments more valuable and meaningful. Although I pray never to have to relive that time of depression, I have to acknowledge it's contribution to who – and where – I am today.

CHAPTER 17

The Search Is Over

I'll bet that most people probably feel their family and their religion are two resources they can turn to for guidance and for comfort. I never had the opportunity to develop those feelings for the family I had been born into, and my recent church experience left me feeling spiritually bereft.

But, I still had my saving grace – Peaches. She didn't make empty promises or turn away from me when the going got tough. She worked through the obstacles with me; it was she who dug deeper into the real roots of my depression and again suggested that I look for my family.

I thought about it, while I also continued to concentrate on the business, which became a sort of refuge for me. Throughout that terrible time of depression and despair, I had somehow managed to hold on to my business, which was, in fact, actually starting to grow. I'd bought my first van, hired my first employee, and was off and running.

Eventually, it dawned on me while sitting in my office one day that the skills I had developed in business could be very useful in my personal life as well. I was winning contracts by writing proposal after proposal, which involved doing a lot of research and finding the right sources for different supplies and employees. If I was able to find information and figure out all of these things, why wouldn't I be able to I figure out where my mother was? She was really the focal point. My search was all about finding my mother.

I decided to use what had helped me become successful to take another stab at finding her. Not just my ability to research, but the traits of determination and perseverance. Peaches wouldn't let me give up on myself when I was going through hell, and now I wasn't about to give up on what I had been looking for, in one way or another, my entire life.

Before, I had just flipped through the Yellow Pages, calling anyone with the same last name. It was an inefficient, half-hearted approach, which was not how I ever went about things at all. This time, I decided to use a more methodical process.

I placed a call to the agency responsible for handling birth and death records in Washington, D.C., to find out if I could get a copy of the birth certificates of those people whose names were listed on my own birth certificate – specifically, my mother and my father. I managed to obtain a copy of my mother's certificate and searched to find another agency that could tell me whether she was still alive.

To my surprise, every agency I contacted was extraordinarily helpful when they learned what I was trying to do. I had anticipated a long, drawn out, difficult process, but people were very receptive and really wanted to help me. It's amazing what the understanding and support of others can do for the human spirit. I felt recharged, with each bit of information like a piece of a puzzle, leading me to who I needed to search for next.

When I was told that there was no death certificate on file for Dorothy Lee Upshaw, I had one of my most important questions answered. My mother was alive. I stumbled across another government agency – possibly the Department of Child Welfare – and told them a bit of my story. The agent on the other end of the phone told me that if my mother had been anywhere in the system, in any capacity whatsoever, he could probably help me find her. Two short days later, that agent called me back. Though he did find some information, he could not legally *tell me* where my mother was. He could, however, send a note *to her* telling her where I was.

This moment was the closest I'd been to my mother since I was thirteen years old. For so many years, I had no idea whether she was dead or alive, living around the corner or around the world. And I had no idea whether she knew anything at all about me. I don't know how I made it through those days of waiting once the agent sent that letter. I imagine it's like waiting for a lab result on a biopsy. You just want the waiting over and to know what you're dealing with.

But, all I could do was wait – and hope. After a few days, my receptionist told me I had a phone call from someone with the IRS.. Nobody wants to unexpectedly hear from the IRS, and I was very hesitant about taking that call. The young lady on the other end identified herself as Cynthia Rawls, and then asked if the letter she had received in the mail was a joke. The question was mutual on my part since I didn't know what she was talking about. She explained that she worked for the IRS, but that the call was of a personal nature. She thought she might be my sister.

This may not have been the phone call I was hoping for, but I thought I was closer than ever to the end of my search. I've since learned that even when you physically find what you're looking for, it doesn't necessarily mean the end of your quest. What's that expression? Life's a journey, not a race to the final destination. Maybe it doesn't go exactly like that, but the point is to keep living, keep searching, keep improving and keep positive. Just keep on keeping on.

It turned out that Cynthia lived in the apartment once occupied by her mother. She had been the one to open the letter the agent had sent a few days earlier. She vaguely recalled hearing about other siblings when she was younger, but no one ever talked about it as she got older. She was as overwhelmed with emotion as I was, and started screaming and hollering with excitement. She just couldn't believe it.

We talked about the rest of the family - and we decided to call the siblings we knew on both sides.

While in the Army, I had stayed in touch with my siblings who had also been placed in foster care, so I knew how to reach them. Yvette had done some research of her own about our siblings during those years. While I got in touch with those who had grown up in foster homes. Cynthia called the others. We planned a get-together at our oldest sister's house a couple of days later. I was also told that my mother would be there.

I'm sure I had mixed emotions, but all I can remember is looking so forward to that day. It couldn't come fast enough for me. The impromptu family reunion was a big shock – for everyone, I'm sure – but it was also exciting. We were eleven children in all - Pearl, Derek, Denise, Dennis, Olivia, Cheryl, Yvette, Cynthia, Renee, Joe, Anita.

The youngest of my mother's children went by the last name, Upshaw. My mother's name. Along with Renee and Cynthia, they were part of this second group of children my mother had and raised, after she'd put me and my other siblings in an orphanage. Derek and Pearl, my oldest siblings whom she kept, still had a relationship with my mother as well.

I felt then, and still feel to this day, a sort of divide between all of us. There will always be a separation between the foster-care kids - Denise, Olivia, Cheryl, Yvette and me - and the rest of them. My mother had never told any of her other children about the kids she had given up. Derek and Pearl were the only ones who knew about both sets of kids, but I'm still not clear whether they had *decided or were told* not to say anything to the second group.

How is a person supposed to feel when he walks into a room full of people that are his family and doesn't know most of them? When he sees the face of the mother he hasn't spoken with in more than twenty years? The woman he has been searching for really since she left him at that orphanage.

I helped to initiate this gathering at my sister's home, and was willing to do whatever it took to make it a positive, fulfilling experience for myself. It had taken a long time, many bad, and some good decisions, a lot of pain, sadness and suffering, more than an ounce of courage, strength and determination, and the unending love and support of an amazing woman to get to this moment in my life.

My mother sat in a chair against a wall, a look that I can only describe as "reserved" on her face. No big, welcoming smile. No "So happy to see you," greeting. She seemed to be more serene - and sad. Thinking back, I realize she was probably more in a state of shock than anything else.

Each of her children approached her, one by one. Some had been in the same situation I had been in, others weren't even aware of our existence.

My mother's body language said it all. It had to have been a difficult moment for her, emotionally. She hugged each of us, individually, and told each of us, individually, that she loved us. Verbally expressing her love for her children was apparently something my mother had taken to doing in her later years, and I heard the words often after that first occasion. I never once took them for granted.

Hearing the words "I love you" from your mother probably ranks high on the list of things people, especially kids, take for granted. And then, one day they wish they could hear that voice and those words just one more time. I didn't have quite so normal a childhood; those words weren't often spoken to me – and certainly not by the mother I had not seen.

That first time, after more than twenty years without contact – verbal or visual – is a moment that will forever be seared in the emotional memories of my heart. I choke up thinking back on that moment to this day.

I did make a conscious effort to work on building a relationship with her after that. I had longed for her, prayed for her to come back, during most of my childhood, and I thought that after waiting for this most of my life, there would be an instant and natural connection.

Sadly, but I guess, naturally, that was not the case. I had to work to love her, and work to forgive her. The conflict of emotions went on in me for more than ten years, but I was excited that I had found her. I did not regret it, and though it wasn't an easy process, nothing worthwhile ever is.

Before I had found my mother, I would speak at my church on Mother's Day and share my dilemma about my own mother with the congregation. I didn't know whether she was dead or alive, and because of that, I didn't know how to engage in the celebration. I had felt like I was in limbo, not knowing whether I was mourning a mother who'd already passed or celebrating one who was still living. At least now, I knew.

Not everything I learned was easy to deal with. In addition to being a mother to other children after giving me away, my mother was apparently also now a community-involved, church-going woman. She had a second set of children who knew only this side of her life, and nothing of her other life as the person she was when she was *my* mother. Naturally, my siblings' perception of her was totally different from mine. It was really hard to reconcile this woman with my own memories and image of the woman who was my mother.

It is an ongoing battle.

CHAPTER 18

More Than I Bargained For

At that first reunion at my older sister's house, I realized that although my sister had the same last name as me, "Harris," all of my mother's kids who had been in foster care were apparently really "Scott." The other, second group of my mother's children had different fathers altogether. Even today they still haven't figured out who their fathers are, except for Joe.

My older brother, Derek, had pulled me aside during the reunion and told me that he knew where my father, Oscar Lee Scott, was. At this point, the rest of my siblings didn't know if Scott, which is what we called him, was actually their father or not. But, my older brother strongly believed that he was and thought I should meet him.

Derek called my father right then, from my sister's house, and my father ended up coming over that night. It was extremely awkward, and we greeted one another very formally. A handshake, not a hug.

My original and sole purpose for this search that had been the theme of my life for so many years stemmed from my desire to simply find my mother. I never imagined I would uncover so many brothers and sisters, and my father, and even more siblings. It wasn't something I could emotionally prepare myself for, and juggling all these feelings about all these new people in my life would take effort. I'd faced bigger challenges, and I suppose the expression, "Be careful what you wish for, you just might get it," would apply well to my life at this point. I had wished long and hard for a family of my own, and boy, did I ever find one.

Before we left that first get-together, all the siblings decided we'd have a more formal reunion. We held it at the park near the first house Peaches and I lived at 1109 Elsa Ave., Landover Maryland. We must have been quite the sight, but then again, maybe we were the picture of what a family reunion looks life. It was a huge spectacle, with all of these adults and even more kids. We hauled in a tremendous grill and generators on a trailer. We played volleyball, the kids played in the playground. It was a good, old-fashioned family picnic.

We were all fresh and new to one another, so naturally we were all hugging and loving and happy. We didn't know each other well enough yet not to be. On the surface, things always appear to be fine, but what divides people doesn't generally come out until they begin to dig a little deeper, expand a little further.

I remember that around the time that I was getting to know my siblings, an infamous incident occurred in Los Angeles, where four police officers had beaten a black man, named Rodney King, for resisting arrest. The officers, who were white, hadn't known that the entire incident was being filmed by someone with a video camera. There was so much racial tension resurfacing at that time – maybe it never really went too far away to begin with. When the cops were acquitted, mass riots broke out, causing a billion dollars in damages and leaving more than 50 people dead. When feelings boil below the surface, they will eventually erupt.

Race isn't the only factor that separates, divides and causes turmoil. Religion, social status and nationality can all do the same. So could my unique family situation.

Though early on, we'd attempted get-togethers on a regular basis, at almost every opportunity, someone would use this time to bring up the past. There were always moments of bad feelings, some that boiled over. Because of that, the get-togethers started waning. Nobody wanted to be in that type of negative environment.

Two of my sisters had decided from the beginning to hold a grudge against my mother. They were very negative about what she had done. I was very into church and forgiveness at the time, and tried to make an appeal to them about how life can throw you curves and not to be judgmental. That was my perspective at the time.

Cheryl, the baby of the foster care group, still refuses to have anything to do with any of us.

I often remember all of the days that I prayed to have a family of my own. I realize, now, that this is what a family is. Not some big dream where everybody gets along and is happy all of the time. But this was a bit more difficult, because many of us really didn't know one other. That brought a little animosity into the mix.

Those who didn't get to grow up with the rest resented it a little. The second group of my mother's children and the older kids who didn't go into foster care knew things about each other. They connected in ways that the rest of us couldn't. We were still trying to figure out who we were to each other; they already knew.

We even talked about going on Oprah to share our story, and way back then, I said that I was going to write a book about our family story one day. Though my siblings all encouraged me then, I'm not so sure everyone will be thrilled about it now. Man, how relationships have changed.

I guess we really have become a family over the years – with all of the mess and drama that comes along with it.

CHAPTER 19

Risky Business

All the while I was discovering my old family, exploring relationships and emotions that were new to me, I was also still working hard at building my business.

Since I'd first discovered *Black Enterprise* back in the Army, I'd remained a regular subscriber. The magazine became my guide for how I should look and how I should interact with people, particularly in business. One of the things I looked forward to most was their annual list of the top 100 African-American-owned businesses in the country. One of the criteria for making the list was achieving $5 million in revenue. One company was local, with $10 million in revenue – and they worked in telecommunications. Here I was, trying to get to $50,000, with a goal of earning $250,000 in revenue. Those numbers in the millions seemed so far out of reach.

But I was so impressed by that local company that I decided to be brave – again – and write to their president, asking if he'd meet with me. Just like all those years ago, when I'd reached out to Earl Graves at *Black Enterprise,* I figured it was worth taking a chance. The man agreed to meet me, and I nervously but excitedly prepared for what might be my next big step.

Although I owned my business, at that time I was basically still a technician, with one van and one part-time employee who I had to pick up and drive home every day. I was the guy in jeans doing the physical work. Now here I was, all cleaned up, in a suit and tie, about to have a meeting that I hoped would change my prospects. When I entered that corporate office and saw all of those professional, well-groomed people, I thought, "That's what I want to be when I grow up."

During that meeting the owner shared his business philosophy with me, and some of what he said still impacts the way I do business today. I'd approached him as the little guy who wanted to become his subcontractor. But his philosophy was that he didn't sub out his own work; instead, he presented his company to even bigger ones as their subcontractor. He basically used his credentials to attract larger businesses that needed his services.

That philosophy really impressed me then and has always stayed with me, until today. He and I remained in touch over the years, and when my business eventually reached – and passed – the million dollar mark, we even collaborated on a couple of jobs.

Based on what I'd learned from him, I began reaching out to other similar companies in the area, looking for partnerships and joint venture opportunities. I became aware of contracts that other companies were working on. When those contracts came up for bid, I submitted my own proposals. Now I was really in the game, offering competition to other companies. This was all perfectly acceptable; there was nothing unethical about submitting a competing bid. It's just the way business is done. In fact, we business owners all felt that the competition was good for the business community in general.

Basically, I was networking with Prince George's County business owners. Everything I've ever read about being an entrepreneur and marketing your business says that you can't underestimate the value of networking. From my experience, I believe this wholeheartedly. There may be no better way of learning about new opportunities than by interacting personally with other business owners.

One company in my network had never subcontracted their work, but decided to sub to me for the first time. My company, TSC, was awarded a contract to upgrade the wiring in all 127 schools in the Prince George's County system.

This was a huge contract, one that I felt could really propel my business forward. Once again, Peaches believed in me and agreed to help me secure a $10,000 line of credit from the bank – we signed over our house as collateral. This was not an easy thing to do – basically, I was putting my family's future on the line. But with Peaches' support and my own determination and belief in what I could do, I knew it was a risk we had to take.

Now I was lead technician, project manager, and finally, actually running a company – handling payroll, managing employees, scheduling work, and everything else that's involved in running a business.

With all this growth, I decided to move to a bigger location, and I really dug in and focused on building the business. Always looking for new ideas, I learned that the state of Maryland required majority-owned companies to subcontract work to minority-owned businesses. Recognizing this as a tremendous opportunity, I marketed my company to a big telecom firm that installed phone systems for the state. They had revenue of about $50 million, and they awarded me an 18-month subcontract.

Those 18 months went very well, and I was thrilled when the company offered to formally include me in their next bid proposal to the state – for a five-year contract.

They won the bid, and TSC was awarded 20 percent of their $5 million contract, in keeping with the state's requirements. Now, this was truly huge. I rented a brand-new office space that I had fit out for my company, and splurged on renting nice office furniture, like wooden desks and leather chairs.

With this new contract, my annual revenue was in the half-million dollar range, and growing. I had about 15 technicians working for me, with five trucks covering the state of Maryland, and a secretary and an accounting firm to help with the books.

It looked like I was really on my way toward meeting my business goals. I was determined to keep at it, to do whatever was necessary to keep on this path. I knew it would take hard work. In economic terms, 1991 was a kind of scary year. The US was involved in the Gulf War, and war always impacts the economy. The country was in a recession, and everyone was worried about interest rates and inflation. Entrepreneurs were particularly concerned – we all knew that so much of our success depended heavily on the overall economic outlook.

And sure enough, eventually the shaky economy hit me. There came a point where I had enough money to either pay my guys or pay the taxes. I chose the guys. This decision left me owing close to $20,000 in quarterly taxes. In addition to that, I had gotten a $20,000 bank loan (after repaying the original $10,000 line of credit), and had also borrowed money from a state-run line of credit for small businesses.

I owed a lot of money. And to make matters worse, my major customer, the company that had awarded me my big contract, filed bankruptcy. This was clearly not good news for me, and if I let it, it could have been the end of everything I'd worked toward.

Now, if you've been keeping up with the story, you know I wasn't about to just let that happen. No way. Of course, I was worried. My family's wellbeing was at stake. I knew that I could always get a job with a company again, but I wasn't going to give up on my own business.

Even though I was still going through a terrible depression, I persevered where business was concerned. In some ways, I think work was the one thing, aside from Peaches, that helped me.

After a lot of thought and prayer, I decided to look for a partner, figuring that maybe someone with some capital could buy part of the company. When I look back now, I realize how huge that decision really was. I'd had a lifetime of being disappointed by people – my mother, my father, my pastor – and now I was willing to take a leap of faith and trust a virtual stranger with something as important as my livelihood.

But I knew what was important to me. I'd worked very hard to make a success of my business, and I accepted what I had to do to keep it alive.

Although this was a difficult time, it didn't crush my dream, not by a long shot. Quite the opposite, in fact. My vision was no longer to make $250,000; now I wanted to make $1 million in revenue. I even printed a flyer that said, "This year I will get to $1 million," and put it on my dashboard, on the bathroom mirror, on my office wall. Everywhere I went, I saw that statement – I wanted to be constantly reminded of it all the time.

I met with a business owner from Connecticut who was interested in finding a company that participated in the Small Business Administration's SBA-8a program, in order to gain access to federal work. I'd applied for and been accepted to SBA-8a, a nine-year program in which the SBA positions minority-owned businesses to get additional resources and contracts, in an effort to level the playing field.

We thought the two companies were a good match and talked about what kind of goals we had – I was thinking about $1 million; they were thinking of multiple millions.   We made a hand-shake deal. I was elated. Little did I know that it was probably the worst hand-shake of my life.

I believed that I was taking the right step, heading for better things. I moved again, into a bigger office, with a bigger warehouse and storage space, and began rebuilding the company and the team.

The Connecticut company was focusing on a multi-million dollar deal with the US Navy, in Charleston, SC, and needed the SBA-8a participation to help them get this huge deal. I spent time at their Charleston office, glad-handing around the Navy base, becoming the face of the company.

I was able to take a salary, one good enough that Peaches and I decided we could afford to move to a bigger house. In fact, we went from thinking about looking at a bigger house to actually building our dream house. We moved into it in 1996, just some six months after the birth of our fourth child and only son Donovan.

This was quite a time for me. I felt successful in business, and was very happy with our new home. I was taking overnight trains to Charleston, riding in a sleeper car, going to the office I now shared with the other company. After about a year of traveling once a month, we finally won that big Navy contract.

Here I was, finally taking a six-figure salary, and wondering if I would become a millionaire now. I was feeling very good, to say the least. Once again, work was offering me a reprieve from my state of depression.

But all good things come to an end, as the saying goes. This great deal wound up being very expensive. We were paying high salaries, burning through money like crazy, trying to capitalize on this $30 million contract.

In the meantime, with all the additional capital I now had, I'd built TSC up to revenue of more than $2 million. I was making great money, living in a 5,000 square-foot home in a gated community. My entire perspective on my life and all that I'd been through was changing. The hard work was really paying off.

One thing that's certain in life is change – and it isn't always good. About a year after we moved into our new home, the Connecticut investor who had been financing my company got impatient with the process. He decided he wanted out.

While this was happening, I was in the midst of losing my connection with my church. The one place that should have been my solace had become a place where, once again, I felt I didn't belong. I was struggling mightily to fight through the worst depression I'd ever known, and I'd lost the central focus of my faith. In addition, the work that had always been my refuge was now causing me great worry.

CHAPTER 20

Starting Over

By the late 90's, the investors and I finally just fell out. The main investor was demanding repayment of the money we'd used, which was around $700,000. This was not good news.

I thought hard about how I could get out of this situation. Once again, I decided to take a step that I'd never anticipated. I contacted a company I knew through my networking, asking if they'd be interested in buying TSC. They hired an accountant to go through my books and structure a deal.

In 1999, I sold 90 percent of TSC to QTSI (Quality Telecommunication Services), which averaged $3 million in annual revenue.

Since the owners were retired from the Air Force, most of their work was at Air Force bases around the country. They purchased TSC to help them secure commercial and local government telecom work. I retained ten percent ownership and ran the new Commercial Division that I had created for their company.

Within four years we had grown that company from $3 million to $12 million in revenue. In 2002, they had the biggest profit they'd ever had, about $1.2 million in cash profit.

But some lessons are hard learned. Once again, we made the mistake of getting too excited. They rewarded me for increasing their revenue by leasing a Mercedes-Benz ML-500 for me. It was a top of the line, fully loaded SUV, with leather interior, navigation system, and every luxury you could think of. And obviously, ridiculously expensive.

I began to feel like a totally different person. I would lie in bed at night, staring up at the massive tray ceiling in my huge master suite, trying to connect with who I *thought* I was. You'd think I'd be over the top with happiness, but I was struggling with whether I deserved all of this. The fact that I'd worked hard – very hard – didn't seem to penetrate my brain. Inside, I was still little Dennis, the boy who wasn't good enough.

Although I was feeling successful and had all the trappings that you'd think would make a person happy, I still suffered from my underlying depression. I couldn't help wondering when I'd lose it all. I guess you could say I was nervously successful, too scared to fully enjoy what I'd earned. If I didn't really deserve it, then surely someone would eventually take it all away.

And as it turned out, I had good reason to be nervous. When QTSI bought their portion of TSC, I was paid a lump sum of $75,000. This went directly to the Connecticut investor I was indebted to, and QTSI was obligated to submit quarterly reports and $5,000 per month to satisfy the remaining debt.

The accountant who structured the buyout deal was hired as our CFO, and put together a payment structure for those payments. All three of us principals closed our eyes and left him to handle the details. That was a big mistake. After making the first two or three payments, he started falling behind on filing reports and making the payments. Naturally, the investor became suspicious and decided to take us to court.

The lawsuit forced us to file bankruptcy for TSC, which still existed as a division of QTSI. I still owned my first home, which I rented out for additional income. Because it was part of the collateral on the deal with the Connecticut-based investor, I also had to file personal bankruptcy. I just knew that eventually the bottom was going to fall out. How could it possibly not, with all this going on?

Fortunately, our current home wasn't affected. I don't even know how I would have reacted if I'd thought that I'd lost my family's home. I was torn up enough over some of the decisions I'd made and having to declare bankruptcy – I wouldn't have been able to forgive myself if I'd lost the house, too.

On top of all this, QTSI went into a tailspin, losing contracts and revenue. In trying to reverse the downward spiral, they brought in a consultant to review the company and make recommendations for improvement.

He decided that my best role would be as a salesman, not as Vice President of Sales. Now, that wasn't going to work for me since I had been promised a small equity position in the main company, QTSI, and remained a shareholder in TSC, guiding it through the bankruptcy filing. It was an insult to take a sales position.

So now I had some ego and pride thrown into the equation. I just couldn't bring myself to take that step back, and decided to leave QTSI. Between the severance I was owed and what I'd saved up, I had three or four months worth of money to work with. After a couple of weeks of lying low, licking my wounds, I started thinking about what to do next.

Once again, I entered a period of deep thought and introspection. Did I want to continue what I'd been doing? Was it time for a change? I considered my own needs, and of course what would be best for Peaches and our children.

In the end, I decided that I wanted to work as a consultant. I put my old list-making skills to work and assembled a set of criteria for selecting a company that I'd like to work for.

I spent long nights at the computer, e-mailing my credentials to companies that were new in the SBA-8a program, offering my experience to help them win government contracts.

Sunglow Technologies, a telecommunications company from California, was intrigued and asked me to meet with them. While this was certainly good news, I absolutely hated flying. I'd had a couple of bad flight experiences and really didn't want to do it. But too much was at stake to let anxiety make the decision for me. I sucked it up, overcame my fear and made the trip.

Good thing I did. Sunglow hired me to open an east coast office use my local contacts to go after business for them.

I realized that I was building a career pattern. As they say in business, I'd found my niche – taking companies further than they could go on their own resources.

And again, this good thing had to reach its end. Within a year I'd grown the new office to such an extent that Sunglow couldn't fund it. They decided to back away from their east coast plan. Within a year of landing the job, I was unemployed again.

CHAPTER 21

Finding My Father

During the weeks following the first family reunion at my sister's, I attempted to contact my father. I wanted to establish some sort of relationship with him, figure out what had happened in the past, and get to know him. It seemed like a logical continuation of finding my family.

Our relationship took a while to develop – in part because I probably didn't go about it the right way.

In trying to get to know him, I learned that he was highly regarded in his community, had been a Boy Scout leader, and was well respected in his church. Ironically, I had also been a scout leader, a deacon in my church and was doing rather well, at the time, in the business that I had begun from the ground up.

This only served to stir up feelings of anger and bitterness in me. I was unknowingly living a life to similar to the one he had lived. But, I was nothing like him. I valued my family. Never in a million years could I fathom walking away from them, abandoning them, or not trying to find them if they were taken from me.

Though I couldn't reconcile this respectable image my father had in the community with the man who never once visited me while I was in an orphanage or foster home, for some reason I did still seek his opinion about business while we were trying to reconnect. Uncle Ollie had been the only true father-figure I'd ever had, and I'd learned a lot from him in my younger days about finances and business – and about being a family man, too. But I guess I never outgrew wanting the advice of my father. Or maybe I just wanted the actual opportunity to seek his advice.

He did have some influence on my thoughts and decisions. Working for the U.S. Naval Research Lab for more than thirty years, he was exposed to a lot of innovative, technologically advanced minds. During his years there, the world's first satellite tracking program and GPS were invented, among many other things.

During our attempts to reconnect, I pressed my father about what happened when I was just a little boy. Why didn't he ever come to see me when I was living in that orphanage? Where had he been all those years I lived there and in foster care? How could he not come to see me?

According to my father, when he came for his usual weekly visit with me and my siblings at the boarding house, we weren't there. He asked my mother where we were, but, again, according to him, she wouldn't tell him. My mother did tell him that she warned him through the years that all of us were too much for her, and that he just didn't listen. That was the extent of his answer.

Did he ever try to find me? How hard did he look, if at all? Answers I don't know, will never know, and maybe don't want to know. Because he is my own father, I can judge him as harshly or kindly as I choose. His actions affected me, so I am entitled. But, he wasn't alone in his absentee fathering, as African-American leaders from Dr. King and Jesse Jackson to Bill Cosby and even Chris Rock have pointed out in their own insightful ways. And the most significant black male to rebuke black males for their lack of presence in their children's lives – Barack Obama:

"…what too many fathers also are is missing - missing from too many lives and too many homes. They have abandoned their responsibilities, acting like boys instead of men. And the foundations of our families are weaker because of it. You and I know how true this is in the African-American community.…We need fathers to realize that responsibility does not end at conception. We need them to realize that what makes you a man is not the ability to have a child – it's the courage to raise one.… more than half of all black children live in single-parent households, a number that has doubled – doubled – since we were children."

His speech in 2009 is a sorry reminder of how much company my father had – and still has – in the black community today.

During an impromptu visit to my office one day, my father indicated that I must want something. I was happy that he had stopped by, but was still harboring some anger about the past. In a sense, he was right. I did want something. But I could never get what I really wanted. I wanted my father. Here he was standing in front of me, in my life, yet what I wanted was him in my past. I wanted him to have been there for me. And then I got angry. He was suspect of me? This wasn't some gold-digging venture for me. I was doing perfectly fine in my life and in my financial abilities to take care of myself and my family. I lost my temper a bit at that point and shouted, "Look around. Does it look like I need anything from you?"

I decided to write him a letter after that, to let him know what it was that I really wanted – for his grandchildren to know who he was, and for he and I to get to know one another. If I had left it at that, it probably would have been okay.

But, I issued a threat to expose him to the church and to the community that held him in such high regard. What would they think of him if they knew who he really was?

I was pretty unyielding; but really I was trying to get closer to him. I ended up scaring him away instead. Threats never go over too well. .

It took probably three years with little, if any, communication before we could relate to one another. He wasn't totally convinced that I was really his son. After another family reunion, I wrote to him asking if he would agree to a DNA test. I wanted to be convinced, too.

He agreed, and I met him at his house on a Sunday after church. Even as a child, I had never been to the house he lived in. So the first time I ever visited my father's house was to establish once and for all that he was in fact my father.

I had bought a DNA kit and done the research on how to conduct the test. I am nothing if not efficient in my perseverance. I attempted some idle chit chat, but he wanted to get it over with, so I took a swab from his mouth and left.

When I called him with the results confirming that the match was 99.9 percent, I told him, "I guess I can call you dad now." His reply was that he was glad I got the information I had been looking for.

We communicated occasionally over the phone, and he once invited me on a fishing trip. Me being who I am, always wanting more, I ended up being a bit disappointed because it wasn't just the two of us on the trip. He had invited my younger brother, older brother, and my sister's husband, as well. I think that fishing trip ended up being the only thing I'd ever done with him in my life.

I had never really consciously thought about finding my father; my quest had been all about my mother. I was curious about his name being different from mine on the birth certificate, but finding my father was more of an afterthought than a priority. Once I found him, though, I became sort of obsessed with getting to know him.

I learned that he was born on November 4, 1925 in Montgomery, Virginia, the older of two children. He grew up in Washington, DC, in the Shaw community, where he graduated from Garnette Patterson, Jr. High School and Armstrong High School. He served in the US Army during World War II, and worked for thirty-six years at the Naval Research Lab.

His obituary says,

"Scottie loved fishing, hunting, camping, traveling, singing and telling jokes. He served as a referee for the DC Department of Recreation and was once in the early 50's a member of "Earl and the Boys" singing group. He was married to Gaynel for nearly forty years, and was an active member of the renowned Metropolitan Baptist Church for over fifty years. One could always find him volunteering to help in any capacity."

We had traveled similar paths in terms of our life decisions – he was a scout master, highly respected in his church, an entrepreneur. He was even in a singing group.

So was I. But he was married to another woman while having all of these kids with my mother. I wear my father's retirement ring to this day; the ring he received from the company he worked at for more than thirty years. The US Naval Research Lab that was right on the other side of the highway from where I lived in D.C. Junior Village for too many years – the place that he claims he had no idea about. I didn't fully trust his answers then when he told me, and am not convinced, even now, that he didn't know where I was.

We did manage to get past most of the things that were blocking us from developing a relationship – other people and our own issues. Overcoming the emotional obstacles helped me to dig myself out from a lifetime of feeling abandoned – which impacted most of my life decisions – to feeling like I really did belong to something and to somebody. I think I felt like I found my place when I found, and essentially forgave, my father.

On the other hand, I also feel like I never really got to know him. I missed what made him great in his community. He was older, retired, and shortly after I came to know him, hospitals and nursing homes became a way of life for him.

While he was in the nursing home, I arranged for my personal barber to visit and give my father a shave and haircut. I wanted to do something special for him as a surprise. I'll never forget how proud my father was of that experience, bragging to every nurse that walked into his room about what his son had done for him. That's always stayed with me.

A lot of children take their parents and the things their parents do for them for granted. A lot of children give back to their parents later on in life, remembering how much their parents did for them in their earlier years. My father didn't give me a foundation, values, ethics or a family life when I was younger, but I think he gave me the knowledge that my inner sense of self came from somewhere. In the end, I did feel connected to him. We even looked almost exactly alike.

But, I regret that I never did get the real essence of the man – the man I knew he was from talking to my older brother and sister – and I am left longing, still.

CHAPTER 22

MORE SIBLINGS

My reunion with my father led to a connection with still more siblings.

I learned that I had three other sisters – Peggy, Roxanne and Brenda. Each of them had their own mothers. My father, we called him Scott, was married to his wife for more than thirty years before she passed. In my calculation, most of the time that he was married to this woman, he was also having children with my mother – and other women. Ironically, he and his wife had no children of their own.

My older brother, Derek, set up a meeting between me and Roxanne, the youngest of my father's three daughters, and the most open and liberal of all of them. Unlike Brenda and Peggy, she was very willing to meet me and get to know me. She's since moved to North Carolina, where Derek lives, followed by my sister, Denise. My sister Pearl and her husband, Darden, have also moved there, to his hometown of Wilson, North Carolina.

After that DNA test established that my father really was my father, and our relationship developed, he sent a letter and check to my oldest daughter, Desiree, for her graduation from Morgan State University. Inside he had also slid a photo of Brenda and her three daughters. I took it as his way of trying to tell me that there were other things I needed to know. But, I was told that Brenda was resistant to meeting me. She thought I should just let everything go. Leave the past in the past. That had not been easy for me to do for many years, but I didn't pursue her. I think I had enough family to handle at that point.

I did end up meeting Brenda while my father was in the nursing home. I visited him often because my office was close by. When she walked in with her husband, there was a look of surprise on my father's face; almost like he'd been caught at something. I introduced myself simply as Dennis. Not "your brother," though I knew who she was. Apparently, he had already talked with them about me. We didn't hug, but shook hands as if we were strangers. I suppose we were. I remember feeling awkward and came up with a reason to leave.

My father had been estranged from his other daughter, Peggy, for years. In fact, he had disowned her because he apparently disapproved of her lifestyle. I wondered how somebody like him, with all of these children and having no participation in their lives, could judge someone else. I wasn't feeling him at all on that and really disagreed with that decision.

I've only talked to Peggy once. Though she had been pointed out to me at my father's funeral, she stayed only long enough to pause at his casket and walked out. I had my father's phone books, so I called her one day. She was shocked. She hadn't even spoken with her sisters for years. I haven't talked with her since, but told her one day I'd figure out a way to invite her to a family event. That's still on my to-do list.

I told Peggy that I wasn't trying to stir up anything, but that I was sort of the "troublemaker" in the family. I was the one who searched for everybody and dug up the past.

I know that a lot of people now probably wish I had left it buried. But, those who don't learn from the past are doomed to repeat it.

CHAPTER 23

ACCEPTING MY PARENTS

By the time I felt at peace with my relationship with my mother, her health was starting to decline. She was, naturally, a totally different person than I remembered as a child. But I hadn't had the privilege of watching her age, so in my mind's eye, she remained the same as she looked when I was a teenager.

My sister kept the family informed of my mother's declining health, which resulted in numerous hospital admissions over a few years, and rounds of phone calls to all of my mother's children. The decision was ultimately made to admit her into a nursing home.

Oddly, this actually gave me the chance to spend more time with her. I was there for her, but was also trying to gain a better understanding of what had gone on in her life in the past, to help me accept and forgive. It was tough. She would break down and cry shortly after we began our conversations, and we never really could get to the substance. Her answers were very "surface level," yet still emotional, and though they never really were to my satisfaction, I did let her know that I loved her and that everything was okay.

I had this sense that my mother was burdened by the gap between her children. She was well aware of the separation between those of us who felt rejected and neglected by her and those who saw her as a Christian lady who was the pillar of her church.

One part of my mother's obituary reads:

"In 1982, she had found her way to church and committed her life to Christ, becoming a member of the Maple Springs Baptist Church where she served as Treasurer of the Senior Citizens Ministry. The children that she did raise described her as lovable, steadfast, fashionable, classy, caring and concerned, willing to help others."

Those that she didn't raise were conflicted, but personally speaking, I felt resolution – maybe even closure – in finding my mother.

I reassured her, to her death bed, that *all* of her children would be okay; that we would get along. To this day, we haven't been completely successful and closed the gap, but we try to tolerate one other, though some siblings refuse to participate in the relationship at all. You can only take responsibility for your own actions – and that itself is difficult enough to do sometimes.

I had wanted my parents to treat me like any other child of theirs, but they were more careful and more formal with me. I had to call them before I went to see them; I couldn't just pop in anytime. I felt like company. We couldn't just sit at the kitchen counter and have a snack. It wasn't that type of environment.

In my own home, sometimes I have to *remind* the kids that I'm their father – they're so comfortable. And, that's a good thing. I know my children and they know me. There's no pretense, no formality. We don't agree on everything, but we've spent enough time together to respect and appreciate each other. You get out what you put in.

My relationship with my mother and father wasn't, and I guess just couldn't be, as relaxed as typical parents and children would be.

My mother passed away in 2003; my father passed in 2004. They were in and out of hospitals and nursing homes at the same time. I was going from different parts of town to visit with both of them, caring for them and trying to resolve my own feelings for them at the same time.

They were the ones who had abandoned me, and yet I was still there for them, although sometimes I had to push myself to be there. It's not easy to admit to these feelings, but to be honest, I had to struggle to get through some of those days. I sometimes put my own family aside to be with them. Now, after the fact, I'm glad that I did it. At the very least, it has helped me to find peace in my relationships with them. But, it was difficult being in the middle of it.

I give all the credit to Peaches, who not only supported me, but accompanied me on many of those visits. She was the buffer to help me get through all of it, from the relationships with my mother and my father, to the ones I developed with my siblings. She is, and has been, the woman behind this man.

From what my parents shared with me, they had their own special relationship. They continued to stay in contact and communicate throughout all those years. Their five children were good reasons for that, though we weren't all always in the picture. Although my parents each had other relationships during and long since their time together, oddly enough, they maintained their own relationship until they died.

By the time I reconnected with them, my parents were in a different stage of life. What I got to share in was when there was little life left. They were different when they were young and vibrant – like most of us – and I missed out on those years. For the most part, I am settled, but still a little empty and conflicted about them.

Sometimes you just need to let go of those things that bring you down, hold you back and keep you stuck. No matter what either of my parents might have said to me, the words could not change my past. It happened. And it happened to me – and to them. And each of us, in our individual lives, had overcome burdens, physical and emotional, to arrive where we were.

CHAPTER 24

Finding My Place

When the Sunglow office closed and it was time to start looking for work – again – I considered working for a company as an *employee* again. After having been a business owner or independent consultant for fifteen years, I was more than a little concerned about what that really meant.

It was important to me that I get to fully use the experience and expertise I had acquired over the years. Once again, I thought long and hard about what I wanted to do, and in the process, I realized something that kind of amazed me. As I reviewed the jobs I'd held, I realized that I really had created my own career. Except for my first job with Rixon (and McDonalds, of course), I'd never taken a job just for the sake of having a job. Every time I needed to find work, I established my own priorities and looked for a specific type of company. It was so empowering to comprehend that I had actually built my own career. It boosted my confidence now that I needed to do it again.

So I made my list. I didn't want to work for a big corporation where I'd be lost in the crowd. I wanted a place where I could impact the bottom line and make a difference, as I'd done at QTSI and Sunglow. I narrowed down a list of ten or fifteen companies, and sent out my updated resume.

All but one of the companies were in telecommunications. I got five interviews from the resumes I'd sent out, and received four job offers from telecom companies. In addition, the one non-telecom firm also wanted to meet with me.

I'd known about Ideal Electrical Supply because QTSI occasionally bought supplies from them, but I had not met the owners. The company was a female minority-owned, husband and wife business, and the husband asked me to meet with him. Though they didn't have an open position to fill, they were interested in me and wanted to hear what I had to offer.

At the meeting, I explained honestly that although I didn't have a background in distribution, my research on their company and the industry led me to believe that I could help them to grow.

They extended an offer after a couple of months, but it was very low in comparison to the offers from the telecomm companies. The thing was, though, I had to admit that I was feeling burnt out in that industry. What I really wanted was to use the skills I'd developed over the years to help a company organize and build their back office and infrastructure. I believed that my expertise could apply to any industry, and I liked the idea of a change.

My salary at QTSI had been six-figures; Ideal's offer was in the mid-$50,000 range. I talked with Peaches, of course, and also with a business associate who called the owners and vouched for me. They increased their offer, but only by a couple of thousand dollars.

This was not an easy decision to make. Accepting the offer would drastically change our lives. Like a lot of people, we had a huge mortgage and, to be honest, we'd grown accustomed to living a bit beyond our means. At this point, we had four children, there were lots of extra expenses for lessons and equipment and such, and I didn't want to deprive my kids of anything. But somehow I believed that this company would give me the opportunity to do even better than I had so far.

One of the deciding factors for me was that the owners were considering their own retirement in a few years, and wanted someone who could take over when that time came. That prospect made the offer even more intriguing to me. It gave me hope that there was a good future for me at Ideal.

After a lot of introspection and talking with my wife, I accepted the offer. But I also made an offer of my own. I'd learned that in its twenty-year existence, the company had never surpassed $10 million in revenue. I took a deep breath and told the owners that I could get them to $30 million in three years. They liked the number, but were understandably skeptical.

We didn't sign a contract, which probably sounds crazy, but there was a lot of trust in the relationship. I started working at Ideal on April 1, 2005. As I was driving to work that morning I couldn't help thinking about it being April Fools' Day, and half wondered if I'd get there to find it had all been a joke.

One of my conditions in accepting the offer was that I'd help in sales as needed, but that my primary focus would not be on selling. Aside from specific business experience, there was also a personal reason for this decision. Over the previous few years I'd developed an anxiety disorder, and often had anxiety attacks when I was out in public.

If you've ever suffered from anxiety, you know that just the anticipation of an attack can bring one on, and I didn't want to start a new job under that burden. I wanted a "safe" place to work, where I wouldn't be under pressure to travel and meet with people on a regular basis. I didn't tell them about the anxiety, but made it clear that I preferred to work in a different capacity. Fortunately, they agreed.

As Vice President of Operations, my job was to oversee the warehouse services and all of the sales force. Basically, I was in charge of everything but the accounting department, which was fine with me. After the stress I'd gone through with my own company and then the bankruptcy, I knew that finances weren't my strong suit. I wanted nothing to do with money, except to draw a paycheck. In spite of this, I did try to learn Ideal's integrated accounting system so that I could gain a more comprehensive view of the company's situation.

As I began to settle in, it didn't take long at all to see that the company was really in a state of disarray. The majority of the sales force did not seem to take their work seriously; it looked to me as if they had no personal investment in the company at all.

In order to do my job, I decided that I needed to get to know both the customer base and the employees. I talked to the staff about what their jobs were really about, which didn't go over very well. They resented the new guy coming in all gung-ho, telling them how to do the jobs they'd become so complacent in. I knew I wasn't going to be making any life-long friends, but unlike them, I did care about the company and took my job seriously.

The more I interacted with the employees, the more I sensed that most of them held a certain disregard for the owners. In a way it's understandable. Although the owners were very involved with the company, they traveled frequently and were often away from the office. I guess "out of sight, out of mind" applies in work as well as any other relationship.

As I said, I knew I wasn't about to win any popularity contests, and within my first year at Ideal, a number of employees resigned. I hadn't been there long enough to know the ins and outs of the relationships among the different levels of staff.

Here's an example of what was going on. I knew one of the salesmen from my last company, and logically thought he would be my advocate at Ideal. Surprisingly, he turned out to be the first employee I had problems with. He had a hot-shot attitude and spent quite a lot of time out of the office. When I told him that his sales numbers didn't match his activity, he got upset and threatened to quit. We wound up involved in an explosive argument, and I basically showed him the door.

After talking with the owners, he apologized to me. And if you're thinking that sounds too good to be true, you're right. None of us knew that after the argument, he had decided to quit. He gave me two weeks notice and continued to work. And before he left, he erased everything on his hard drive – every piece of information related to every single customer.

Needless to say, I learned a huge lesson from that experience. From then on, in a similar situation I would let the person go right away, before they had the chance to do anything vindictive. It's a common policy upheld by many companies to this day, although the reaction in these economically challenged times is that employers are disloyal, cold and insensitive. I guess it all depends on what side of the fence you're standing on at the moment.

One person after another started to resign. I recruited replacements, explaining my vision and goal for the company. I even shared the fact that I'd taken this job instead of accepting one of the higher offers I'd received, just to show my own commitment to the company.

And it worked. It took a few years, but I built a good team.

In the meantime, the accounting system was still an issue, and eventually there was a big blow-up in the finance department. The owners had never granted full access to the system to anyone other than the accounting manager. But I asked for – and received – the password, so that I could see the full picture of where the company stood.

While I needed the information to do my best for Ideal, the accounting manager had good reason to be upset. In short, his department had not been doing everything on the up and up. Fearing discovery, the manager quit, and an audit of the system actually found some illegal activity.

These problems in the finance department left the company struggling, but I continued to persevere in my job. And I succeeded. The first year, I received a $5,000 bonus because the company had grown beyond $10 million, to about $13 million. By my second year, it had grown to $17 million, and continued to increase until it reached $29 million in 2008.

Revenue was just under the $30 million I had projected, and right at the three-year mark I'd set. We broke open some champagne to celebrate. Bonuses increased; my salary was now almost up to what it had been in my previous company. And for the last couple of years it's been back in the six-figure range, with huge bonuses. I'd made the right decision when I accepted Ideal's offer. In spite of the initial uncertainties and problems, I had been able to do exactly what I set out to do – turn the company around, increase its revenue, and advance my own career.

Yet somehow, there always seems to be a challenge waiting for me. In the last year, the company has been thrown back into some turmoil. It began when the owners offered to give me a small percentage of ownership and also hired a man who they wanted to take over when they retire, as a majority owner.

He was hired in 2009 as Chief Operating Officer, which meant he was my boss. In that capacity, he told me that he appreciated what I'd accomplished, and encouraged the owners to reward me for my effort and continue to position the company for future growth.

The owners and I had already talked about loyalty, and in September 2009 they promoted me to Senior VP and gave me the largest bonus I'd ever received. It was great, even though it had big tax implications. Things always look good until the IRS gets involved, but I was still pleased.

The owners asked me to support the new COO's agenda and vision, but despite his initial support, he wanted to bring in an entire new crew. In addition, he wanted to kick the owners out before they were ready to retire, so he could take over. He lasted only six months; during the last five, he and the owners fought nearly every day. I often found myself in the middle, which was not pleasant at all. The new guy was my boss, but my loyalty was to the owners. I wasn't sorry to see him go.

Once the COO was gone, Ideal entered into a recovery period. We're still working on reorganizing and getting things back on track after some of the drastic changes he made. It's a tough period right now, but I think we're still on track to get to our 2011 revenue goal.

Given all the changes, the succession plan for the owners' retirement isn't definitive yet, but they regularly reassure me that I'll be a part of whatever they decide to do. I believe them when they tell me that I'll be protected.

Working for Ideal has been one of the best parts of my career. I'm grateful for the opportunity to use my skills, to contribute to the company and help the owners reach their goals. I'm grateful that they consider me in their succession plan. To this day, we have never needed a contract nor demanded that any intentions be put in writing. I don't think that's very common in business today, but we're fortunate to have an exceptional degree of mutual trust and respect. I hadn't exactly been raised with a sense of trust in other people my entire life, but I've learned enough along the way to know that not everyone lets you down. Some people are true to their word, and even if they're not, you have to be true to yourself.

I've learned some valuable lessons throughout my career. Life is short, and there's a big world out there. In spite of my inherent insecurities and my ongoing struggle with self-esteem, I am confident now that I can do what I have done wherever I go, for any company. I'm enjoying the ride, and accepting whatever rewards my employers give me in their own time.

It's not my company, but maybe one day it will be. Either way, I'm okay with it.

Because of my insecurity, it helps to know that I am appreciated for what I've done. The financial rewards don't hurt, either! I don't have to ask for raises; I'm making more money today than I ever have before.

I believe that the owners and I have kept our word. In fact, I always express the fact that they are true to their word to customers and potential employees. We're still a small business within our industry – our next competitor is in the $100 million range. There's room to grow and I always try to persuade other employees to work as if they have an ownership stake in order to make that growth possible.

As in any business, there are always personnel issues, but I'm pleased with most of my staff. I worked hard to create a positive work environment that everyone seems to appreciate. Some employees have been with us for three years, since the recovery began. I'm happy that they feel committed to the business, and I'm definitely happy that there's much less drama than there was just a few years ago.

Of course, I still subscribe to *Black Enterprise* – I'm sure I always will. Having learned a thing or two about general career improvement over the years, I decided to send a public relations listing about my promotion to Senior VP to the magazine and to some other industry publications. I was genuinely surprised that they all agreed to run the notice; *BE* even asked me for a photo.

You can imagine how I waited for the November 2009 issue. It was almost too much to think about. I bought a whole stack of magazines the day they came out, and when the cashier asked me why I was buying so many copies, I flipped to my picture! She started screaming and carrying on – she didn't even know me, but she sure did make my day!

I used my Facebook page to share my excitement. I wrote a post explaining how I'd first reached out to *BE* so many years ago, and had since modeled so much of my life on what I learned from the magazine. Now, thirty years later, my name was actually listed in its pages.

This was a huge, career-capping highlight for me. In this way, I'd come full circle. The realization of a dream is an amazing thing. It gives you the opportunity to reflect on your accomplishments. I've come so far from that boy in the Army, the kid who first read *Black Enterprise*. Although he's still within me, he's grown up, left his childish ways behind. But that boy had two things going for him – Peaches, and the strong determination to give her the best life possible – and those are the two most important things that have made me the man I am.

CHAPTER 25

Raising My Family

While career success was, and still is, extremely important to me, the answered prayer of my life will always be my own family, the one that Peaches and I have created over the last thirty years. All those years ago, as I lay in bed in D.C. Junior Village, and then in my foster home, I prayed nightly for a family. And for all of the bad that I experienced, there has also been so much good.

The beginning of the "goodness" in my life – after Peaches, that is – was the birth of my firstborn. Desiree came into the world in December of 1980 and really was a love child. Peaches and I had been married and living in our new apartment for barely a year, but we'd been praying for a child. We were newlyweds, very much in love. Maybe other young couples would have waited to have a child, planning until they had enough money or just the right place to live. But neither of us had really known our own parents, so maybe it was perfectly natural for us to be so eager to start a family together. Maybe part of what we wanted was to give our own children the parents we so longed for.

But just because I was excited to become a father doesn't mean that I wasn't nervous. When Desiree was born, I was all of 22 years old. Peaches and I were living in a neighborhood that was nicknamed Dodge City; I was working all the way in Silver Spring, Maryland. We were really just starting out ourselves. And as excited as I was about our baby,

I knew that I didn't have a solid example of parenthood to fall back on. Uncle Ollie and Aunt Bessie were becoming more important in my life every day, and proved to be wonderful role models, but I knew them only as an adult. I was having a *baby!*

I remember speeding around the Beltway to get Peaches to the hospital when she went into labor – like most men, I was terrified of not getting there in time. But we made it, and I was right there for the delivery. I held my wife's hand, but don't think I actually looked at what was going on. It was just too much – but not because of the physical aspect of the birth. I turned my head away, overwhelmed by feelings of love and appreciation, and this honor for Peaches, who was going through so much pain, risking her life, to have this child for me – for us.

Like most new parents, we did everything we could think of to spoil Desiree in our little one bedroom apartment. We surrounded her with love and everything else we could afford to give her. She was a big deal for us.

Her name was actually the name of a friend of mine from high school. We were just friends, nothing intimate, but from the day I met her, I thought she had the prettiest name I'd ever heard. Desiree's name also began another tradition in the Harris family. Peaches' actual name is Doris. With both of our names beginning with D, we got into the pattern of choosing names for all our children that begin with that letter.

I also wanted to honor my younger sister and gave Desiree her name as a middle name. Lavette – who later became Yvette – had the toughest time of all of us in foster care. She had been in an abusive foster home, which has left its impact on her to this day. I think I wanted her to know the same feelings that I had discovered – that she was connected to someone, that she meant something in somebody's family.

For the first four years of her life, Desiree was an only child, and of course, I would do anything for her. While she was in preschool, I was still a cigarette smoker. When I was about 27, a coworker and I attempted to quit smoking, which I announced to the family. Desiree had learned how bad smoking was for you, and said that she didn't want her dad to smoke. I told her that I'd quit, although I was still sneaking cigarettes. She caught me one day while I was sneaking one in the bathroom. I heard her voice on the other side of the door saying, "Dad, I know you're in there smoking. I can smell it." I quit right then, cold turkey – for her.

Desiree was a good mix of Peaches and me, with a sort of steady, even keel personality. But even with all the attention she got, she seemed to lack confidence in herself. She struggled through her early school years, but with perseverance and a lot of help from me, she made it through. She and I had many battles, sitting at the table working on homework. This continued right through high school. I never received a fraction of the help or attention that I gave to my daughter; at her age I was screwing up and learning from my mistakes without the guidance and support that every child needs and every devoted parent gives. It doesn't happen often enough today, for all kinds of reasons. All I know is that I was glad to do for my daughter what hadn't been done for me. Though, I think I ended up turning out alright after all.

When Desiree started college, her advisors suggested putting her on a special track program. Now, given how hard she and I had worked through all of her school years, I took that assessment as a challenge. I knew what could be accomplished and overcome by working hard, and I was determined to make my perseverance pay off for my daughter.

Not surprisingly, sometimes Desiree became frustrated. In fact, she wanted to quit college in her junior year. I just couldn't imagine getting that far and quitting. We got into it and she was about on the floor in tears, just like I remember her as a little girl, saying she couldn't do it. And I did the same thing I had always done. I told her she could cry, scream and wallow all she wanted, but she was taking her behind back to college. She got her degree in accounting, and when she walked across that stage, it was a proud moment – for both of us. I remember that when we hugged, she thanked me.

Desiree now has two sons, Desmond and Devon. I think she was honoring her mother and me by giving them names that start with D, although she probably wouldn't admit to that. But that's okay; she doesn't need to say it.

My middle daughter is very clear that she won't name any of her children with the initial D, and that's just fine. If there's one thing I've always wanted for my children, aside from knowing that their parents love them, it's a sense of independence. I had too few choices in my life, and I want them to be free to choose their own paths.

Dorian was born in April of 1984, when I was working and traveling, and still at Pleasant Lane Baptist Church. Peaches and I were ordained as deacons about six months after her birth. It was a very busy time.

Now, with two children, I really felt that sense of responsibility weighing on me. And this is the point where reality usually smacks parents upside the head. For a lot of parents, the birth of your first child is an enchanted time, and you feel as though you can spend all of your time just being with your baby. But as that child grows and another comes along, you know that you really have to step up and provide for your family.

Dorian was a beautiful, bubbly, happy child; but I'm afraid that I missed out on too much of her in her baby years. I was always working and was busy with the church, so my focus was divided. I wasn't able to give my full attention at home, and I wish I had been able to reorganize my priorities. I did try, though. Because I never felt I got support on the things that were important to me when I was growing up, I was very sensitive to that with my own children. At least, I thought I was. I showed up for school plays, practices and all activities. Still, I feel that I was too preoccupied when Dorian was little.

She is such a giving and loving person, traits that she inherited from her mother. She looks like Peaches, too. People call them twins; they are that much alike. Dorian is always willing to go overboard and do anything for you. She has always been the very dependable one that we know we can always count on. She and her husband hang out with us, and she's very close to her mother. I'm happy that she wants to spend time with her family.

Dorian took on the role as the baby in the family even though she is the second born, with a few to come after her. She was active in school, involved with both the dance team and the cheerleading squad. She displayed a love for children at an early age and attended childcare classes in high school; we all thought she would end up in the child care profession. She surprised us by getting married at an early age –, just like her mother did. Dorian has spent some time at college and has since enrolled in both nursing assistant and dental assistant training. She seems to be figuring out her way. When she was young, she would stand behind me as I sat, sucking her thumb and twisting my shirt collar. To this day, even as a grown married young woman, she continues to do that. Dorian and her husband Kelvin have become the ambassadors to the rest of the family. They attend nearly every family event on either side to make sure that we are represented.

Donna was born on July 4, 1989. By this time, Peaches and me having children was sort of "old hat." We were still very much in love, but were, after all, ten years into our marriage. We had a routine, and life was good.

But, during Donna's toddler years, I suffered another bout of depression. I was into my new company, TSC, on a full-time basis; it was a struggling business, and I was working hard to keep it going. Peaches was working full-time for the post office as a letter carrier. She was the breadwinner at the time.

Looking back, I feel like Donna came out talking. My wife used to send her in to me while I was lying in bed, blanket over my face, in a dark mood. She'd tell Donna, "Go talk to your dad." In she would come and just start talking. I remember thinking, "She's been here before," as if she were an old soul. Her wisdom and the things she'd say would draw me out of myself, commanding me to talk to her.

While Donna was still little, I rediscovered my love of reading and would go to the bookstore on Saturday mornings, browsing and buying books. I was on the business and self-help track then, and was just reading all the time. Donna would emulate me, always with a book in her hand, even though she couldn't read. She ended up receiving an award for reading one hundred books during the school year while she was in pre-kindergarten! Her reading habits continued into her early teens, and we think it helped to develop her over-achiever mentality. At the same time, she had a bubbly, happy personality, and the family gave her the nicknames Snickers and Giggles when she was growing up.

Donna is one of those people who is just easy to make friends with. She's smart, too, and made her first "B" in eighth grade. Prior to that, she'd been a straight "A" student. She was none too happy about that "B" and wanted me to set the teacher straight for messing up her perfect record. Of course I didn't do that, but explained to my daughter that it was just one of life's realities that she had to accept. Yes, I want to be there to help solve my kids' problems, but there are some lines that even I won't cross. During her growing up years, she would tell her friends that I was her best friend. We played basketball together. She was the first of my daughters to play a sport, probably because of my own thoughts about girls and sports. I guess people would call me a chauvinist, but back then I didn't think basketball was for girls. Desiree had the height and probably should have been the one to play, though.

Donna attends the University of Maryland now and is pretty much the same as she's always been – smart and studying for the LSATs. She should graduate next year with a degree in economics, and then it's off to law school.

In 1996, we finally had our first son, Donovan. Peaches and I figured that by this time everyone was "over" us having kids. Her friends, amazing and supportive women, had thrown baby showers for each of the previous three children. And, true to form, they threw a shower for this fourth child of ours. We were so moved by this, and as I observed Peaches' interaction with her friends and how they all cherished their relationships, I stood up at that shower and told them how I truly appreciated the special friends they are.

I think it's really a testament to Peaches' character and friendship. Me? I have good friends, but I do not think I am a good friend. I've always focused more on what I wanted to achieve, but I've been blessed to have a handful of friends who, in spite of me, have remained very good friends to me. They've allowed me to do what I need to do, and haven't expected me to reciprocate what they've done.

Along with the tradition of giving our children names that begin with the letter D, I had also given them middle names in alphabetical order. I was at the point where I needed a middle name that began with J, and found the name Jakada in a West African book of names. It means "messenger." The name Donovan translates into "dark." He is our dark messenger.

People always make light of my obsession with names, but for whatever reason, they've always been important to me. Maybe it stems from having my name changed in the blink of an eye when I was so young.

Donovan was born during the time when my company was peaking. I'd won the contract with the state of Maryland, had 15 employees, five trucks, and teams of technicians going all over the state. I was so proud going into work in my white station wagon with the company logo painted on it and seeing my company vehicles in the parking lot in front of the office all lined up. It was also then that I learned of the bankruptcy issues with the company I was subcontracting for and hooked up with the investors from Connecticut.

This was also around the time that Peaches and I decided it was time to buy a new house. We'd outgrown our 600-square-foot, one bath, two-bedroom home – there was just no room for Donovan. I described my dream house to Peaches, and she went out with friends looking for it. She found what we wanted in a new development that was being built in a gated community, in southern Prince Georges County, Maryland. We were feeling very successful, but not so much that we felt like we belonged in a gated community! Though we didn't quite qualify for the mortgage, they allowed us to move ahead. This was during more lenient times and the housing boom.

So, Donovan went from a crib in the living room to a 5000 square-foot home in the country. He's never known any other life besides this. His sisters went through the struggling times; they remember when we had to ask the church for money to pay a utility bill or to loan us a heater.

Donovan has grown up thinking that this is how life is supposed to be. The whole community knows him. He has always felt very safe and very free in his neighborhood. He thinks he's the prince of the community. But, all in all, he is a very well-behaved, well-liked young man. He just has the typical thirteen-year-old boy issues. He is an excellent athlete who wants to play and try every sport, and he thinks he's quite the comedian. Between him and Donna, who laughs at anything anybody says, there's jokes and laughter all day long.

Donovan's teachers say it's obvious that he has sisters; he's pretty spoiled. He'll just walk in the door and throw his stuff down, knowing someone will pick it up and put it away for him. I suppose if that's his biggest flaw, we're doing alright. But I don't think his future girlfriends will appreciate that trait.

I sometimes think of him as my alter ego. While I struggle with confidence and hesitate to make a public appearance, he would without delay jump up on stage and perform for a crowd. He loves that attention. I once took him to a Washington Nationals baseball game. At the new stadium in DC they have a Sony Play Station theater where you can load in a song and do karaoke. Donovan jumped up on that stage and went through an entire song in front of the assembled audience and had a ball performing. I just stood there amazed and wished that I had such courage. This is typical of his personality. He recently tried out for his middle school soccer, basketball and baseball teams. Even though he had never played soccer or baseball, he made all three teams.

One of the advantages of having a big house is that we get to have frequent family gatherings, because there's plenty of room for everyone. Those times when all of my children are together, now that many of them are scattered and grown – when they come home for an event, with their significant others and families, I feel the greatest amount of joy you can imagine. I see them together, see how they interact with one other and how well-received and well-respected they are, and it just brings me so much joy. I am overwhelmed by them. I am so very proud of them.

As a parent, it makes me sad that my own mother and father didn't get to feel this about their children. Maybe they did with some of the latter ones, but certainly not with me and my siblings. What wonderful thing they missed out on.

But for me, I really do feel like all the prayers of that little lost child I used to be have been answered. I have led such a blessed life. It all started when I met Peaches, and we began building a life together. We have a good life, and I think it has more than made up for those sad and tough times.

CHAPTER 26

A Foster Family Again

The blessings in my life don't end with the four children Peaches and I made together. Foster care shaped who I am as a person, the decisions that I make to this day, and my longing for my own family. I've always said it was the single biggest impact on my life.

I think it was only logical that after achieving all the success I had in business and all the happiness I had in my personal life, I should want to give back to the system that most affected me. Peaches and I wanted to do something more than just live in a massive house and live a nice life. We were in a perfect position to give back, and so began to research how to become foster parents.

I had plenty of experience and memories of being a foster child, but this new role of parent was one of my own choosing. I wanted to get it right. I wanted to do the best I could, not make some hollow gesture. We began by talking to one of our friends who had already gone the foster parent route. After getting some information, we reached out to the Catholic Charities office that was located right in the community that we both grew up in, on Rhode Island Ave in NE DC, and enrolled in their classes and went through the training.

The one thing I knew right from the start was that I did not want to pick a child by looking at a picture. I guess that stems from my own experience as a foster child. I remember wondering why my foster parents had chosen me based on my picture. It couldn't have told them anything about me or who I really was or what I really needed. Catholic Charities called one evening to tell us about two girls who had been taken in by the city and needed a place to stay. Though we had been thinking in terms of only one child, they knew we had plenty of room, and we said okay.

Brittany was 11 and Shannon about two or three. Like most foster kids, they looked displaced, in a state of shock, uncertain, shy, and afraid. Peaches and I felt right away that we had been given a wonderful opportunity to help. We enrolled them in school, though Brittany had no interest in it at all. She had a real attitude about her, and was still interacting with her mother, who had a substance abuse problem. It was a challenge, to say the least.

But, I was determined not to repeat the pattern of foster parenting that I had experienced. I not only wanted to provide these girls with a roof over their heads and food in their stomachs, I wanted to provide them with opportunity and support.

I remember taking Brittany and Donna shopping to buy Donna a pair of the new Michael Jordan sneakers. She always got the new ones when they came out. Though I did not completely agree with her need to have them, I felt that she earned them with her grades. I am still that way with my children and grandchildren. If you can explain why you need and should have something, I'm willing to consider it.

I asked Brittany if she wanted a pair of Jordan's too, but she picked out an inexpensive pair of shoes instead. When I told her she could pick out two for that price, she got so excited and happy. Doing something as simple as that made me happy too, especially thinking back on how I worked when I was about her age to buy my own special shoes and clothes.

By the time Brittany graduated from high school, she had run for and won class president, and was on the honor roll. She overcame so many obstacles that she could have easily used as excuses to fail. At one point, the agency asked us to adopt Brittany and her sister. We were willing, but wanted to change their names, which Brittany protested against. She felt that we were trying to take her identity away. I can't say that I didn't empathize with her feelings, and I had to respect her choice. I had never been given a choice regarding my name change, and when I finally had one in my middle school years, I refused. So how could I argue her feelings?

Nevertheless, the name change was important to me and my family. Our relationship with Brittany fell apart after that. She asked that they be moved to another foster home that would be willing to adopt her little sister only and just allow he to stay in foster care until she aged out of the system. They were relocated not far from where we live and Shannon was later adopted. Brittany is now a senior at Shaw University. Shannon is in school with Donovan now, and she still runs up and gives a hug when she sees us.

The second group of our foster children was two girls who had been in six foster homes over the previous six months. That should have told us something right there. The social worker basically walked them in, told us to call if we needed her and left. Not usual standard operating procedure. The girls walked right past us and into the family room, and that was the beginning of the end. They lasted with us six months which was longer than they had been with any other placement. These were two extremely undisciplined girls with very vulgar language and equally bad attitudes. We tried to work with them and stabilize them at school. They even cut some other child's hair at school! We kept them until their grandmother finished the foster care program and could take them in.

Shortly after, we became foster parents to two toddler-age children, Tabria and Daquian. They were brought to our house at about 10 p.m. the very night they were taken from their mother. She also had a substance abuse problem.

After about a year or so, we began supervised visitation with their mother. She had been going to all of the required programs, and eventually she did get the children back. She'd also had another baby since they'd come to stay with us.

Less than six months later, the social worker called saying that Tabria and Daquian were back in foster care. Their mother had been arrested and was in the penitentiary. The new baby girl, Quaneice, was also in foster care. In fact, all three of them were in different foster homes.

Peaches and I wanted them, all three of them. Foster care always prefers siblings to be together, so it wasn't too difficult. When those kids walked in, they called us mom and dad like they'd never left.

Somewhere along the line, somebody convinced us to adopt these children. And, why not? I came from quite a big family, though I hadn't grown up with them. So why not expand the size of my own family? On January 20, 2010, we formally signed the petition after four years of being their foster parents. Of course, we changed their names to ones that begin with the letter D. They are part of the Harris family and I want them to grow up feeling like they belong, because they do. Their first names became their middle names.

Danae Tabria Harris is now eight years old and a girl's girl. She is very feminine, likes makeup, fashion, singing, theater and being the center of attention. David Daqoian, seven, is shy, but a typical mischievous boy. He and Donovan seem to have the type of relationship that I envision two brothers should. The type of relationship I might have had with my big brother if we'd been allowed to grow up together. I may have missed out on some things, but I get to watch my boys and that's even better. The baby, Danielle Quaneiece Harris, is five. She has a lot of issues because her mother was using drugs while carrying her, and is being treated with medication to control her over-reactive tantrums. It's not her fault that she was exposed to poisonous chemicals, and we do all that we can to ensure a healthy future for her.

The children are still permitted to see their birth mother, even though their biological family technically doesn't need to know where they are. But we had developed what we thought was a decent relationship with the mother, so we agreed, outside of court, to continue to allow her to visit. The visits seem to have dwindled a bit over time, but she still comes around and we all get along.

All in all, my birth children and my adopted children seem to have a normal family relationship. My other daughters are proud to have these little siblings. My son enjoys the big brother hero worship for the most part.

We all recently attended a Washington Nationals baseball game at Nationals Stadium. We had an amazing family day together, and I'm sure that looking at us, we looked more like a small village. As the lady said, it takes a village to raise a child. And this time, this village is right where I want to be.

As I look back, I am not sure how I arrived at this point in my journey. I started out feeling abandoned and thrown away, having no family and no person in life that I could count on, having to fend for myself, living on the edge and going through difficult and trying experiences. Today, I am a successful, self-made entrepreneur, having overcome obstacles and hurdles and depression, discovered an entire family that I never really knew existed, and reconnected with a mother and father I was never sure I would ever see again. I have been blessed with four absolutely remarkable children of my own, and been able to give to three other children what I missed out on, finally having some sense of belonging and living a truly blessed and amazing life with the love of my life.

As hard as the early times were, everything that I went through served to make me a better person and enabled me to achieve all that I have in my life. I can't imagine what life would have been like if I had ever decided to give up, stop trying and just quit. I am so thankful that I never did.